Praise for The Successful Business Startup Action Guide by Husam S. Alsaleh

"This is an extraordinary book with a different approach to defining a true leader. Good leaders provide direction, purpose, and reason for a group or organization to follow. They also share their knowledge, wisdom, and experience with others. His leadership becomes a calling to serve others. Husam is a natural leader who has risen to a position in his company and industry through actions and words. His thoughts are clear, specific, and on target in today's business and social climate."

Rabi Haout — Serb International Company Managing Director

"Husam combines his competitive spirit, passion for winning, engaging leadership energy, focus on quality, and overall personal programming for success to develop and articulate a proven strategy to start your own venture. This eye-opening, common-sense, and engaging read weaves the perfect balance of stories and frameworks."

Fahad Al-Guthami — Deputy CEO, AmericanExpress Saudi Arabia

"Embracing the message of this timely book won't just add value to your business; it will add value to your life! Husam nails the critical gaps between theory and practicality. This book will have you positively assessing the level of depth in starting your business; it will have you racing into the world to launch your business on your path to personal and professional success. Your status quo will be challenged, but as this driven leader and author points out, 'There are so many business theories that are fluffy. Strategy isn't like that. It's tangible. You can build it like a Lego set.'"

Abdul Ghani El-Ajou — CEO, AlJeel Medical

"Husam puts a new spin on how to start and grow a new business. Husam's book is an easy read that reminds us of the spirit of entrepreneurial thinking. *The Successful Business Startup Action Guide* helps business owners answer some of the most important questions that arise when building a business. An absolute must-read for any business owner or entrepreneur."

Seif Elseif — Managing Director (MD) of Elite Trading Alliance

"Husam Alsaleh possesses all the qualities of a great entrepreneur, and his strategic insights and leadership abilities have led to many professional successes. His intense desire to accelerate his learning velocity—which I have seen him do over the past several years—leads to demonstrable success. Now that he is sharing his stories and insights, all current and aspiring entrepreneurs should immediately buy this book and be ready to take notes.

This read is packed full of insights and lessons from a humble heart and will certainly help many other entrepreneurs on their strategy journeys."

Dr. Rebecca Homkes — London Business School Faculty.
High-Growth Strategy Specialist

The Successful Business Startup Action Guide

Lessons and Mistakes from an Entrepreneur on Building the Future, Starting Businesses, and Leading for Change

HUSAM S. ALSALEH

EMPLOYEE MILLIONAIRE

Employee Millionaire

Limit of Liability/Disclaimer of Warranty:

To Leya, Sara, and Jenna.

Follow your dreams, no matter where they take you.

Contents

Introduction

I Like to Solve Problems

It happens all the time. When I'm in a conversation with a friend and they mention that they are having trouble finding reliable trucks for their business. When I try to get a vehicle repaired and realize that there aren't enough collision repair businesses and the wait for service is too long. When a customer tells me that they want to order spare auto parts online but have been shocked at the cost.

Those moments may seem insignificant when they happen, but sometimes hours or even days later I discover that I'm still thinking about them. Wondering why that problem exists. And thinking about how I might fix it.

This is what it means to be an entrepreneur. Entrepreneurs are equipped with the certainty that a challenge doesn't have to be permanent and the desire to identify how best to correct it.

If you're a bit like me—someone who notices a problem and wants to solve it—then this book is for you. I've spent twenty years in the business world and have served as a board member, a managing director, and a CEO. I've worked in the automotive industry and in warehousing and supply chain management, and I've run a company specializing in quality car repairs. These are businesses that depend on strategic thinking, working in competitive markets, and ensuring continuous customer satisfaction.

I've led my own companies while working in the family business. I've started and scaled several commercial ventures; some have thrived, and others have not.

Like other entrepreneurs, I'm not afraid of failure. I want to fix problems, and I'll try different approaches until I find the best solution. In this book, I'll talk about why some businesses I've launched have taken off while others have struggled. I want to share my story and the strategic expertise of others who've impacted my understanding of what it takes to launch and grow a successful venture. I've learned more from my failures than from my successes. Failure is okay. I've failed often, and I've failed big. I hope that my experiences resonate with you and equip you to better plan and prepare for what's ahead.

So here, at the beginning of this book, I'll share an important secret...

"Business is simple."

Yes, you read that correctly. Too many so-called experts will describe business as an art, requiring a specific, hard-to-achieve combination of skill, years of education, and financial wizardry.

I disagree. I think that a successful business is something you can engineer. You simply need the right strategic framework.

I've spent years developing a strategic framework that is at the core of all of my recent successes. It's been shaped by brainstorming with fellow entrepreneurs, reading deeply, and asking questions of the pioneers who've accomplished great things in the business world.

I'm still learning, still experimenting, and testing these theories, and yes, still failing and gaining knowledge from those setbacks. In this book, I'd like to invite you to join me in learning, researching, and discovering what makes sense for each new business opportunity.

The principles that I use to build a strategic framework have provided a way to test assumptions and ask critical questions. It's a way to make sure that any new business is actually solving a problem that other people want to be solved and that my business is the best one to meet that need. In this book, I'll share those principles so that you can get started on building your own framework. You may have an idea for a business—this book will equip you to begin to test that idea carefully and critically, to determine whether or not it will succeed and what you'll need to do in order to achieve that success. You'll identify the gaps in your knowledge and research that need to be filled. You'll discover how best to move from vision to action. You'll learn how to determine whether your idea will actually be profitable. You'll understand which questions must be answered before you ever approach an investor and which answers are the red flags that should warn you of potential pitfalls.

In this book, we'll discuss the key concepts you'll want to explore—things like market share, industry dynamics, and financials. Most of all, we'll dive deeply into business strategy, equipping you with the understanding of how best to build a framework that you can use for the first business you launch and every business after. I'll share stories from my experiences to show what these principles look like in action and what can happen if they're ignored.

I hope that this book will be helpful to any aspiring entrepreneur who would like to learn from my experiences in starting, operating, and scaling up businesses. I am confident you will find the stories in this book especially helpful to young entrepreneurs who have an idea and a dream of starting a new venture. You may be a recent graduate one or two years into a job. You may be working for a multinational company or a bank to gain experience and begin to raise the capital to launch your business. You may be working in a specific industry because your parents thought it would be a good fit for you, and increasingly you recognize that you want to do something bigger, something that will have an impact in your community, city, country, or the entire world.

I understand that ambition and that energy. Not too long ago, I was in a very similar place. So let me start by telling you a story—a story of my very first entrepreneurial venture.

A Taxi Ride

A little over twenty years ago, I was a student at King Fahd University of Petroleum and Minerals, earning my undergraduate degree in industrial engineering. It was a busy time; I was balancing academic study with working in the family business. It was important to me to be independent and to take action to become more self-sufficient financially. My engineering training was giving me a thorough education in operational efficiency and in problem-solving. I had a lot of ideas on how to run a business better.

I was wrestling with this strong push of ambition during a trip to the UK. A taxi driver was transporting me from one location to another, and we began to chat. He was friendly and very smart, and after talking for a minute or two, I asked him how he had begun driving taxis. He explained that he had not always been a cabbie. He had originally run a business. He and a partner had sold safety equipment to offshore oil rigs; they then trained their customers in how to use the safety equipment they provided.

He described the business model, discussing the challenges he and his partner had encountered in trying to make money from the venture, and the challenges that had ultimately caused the business to fail. I was interested in his model but was far more intrigued by his description of the safety kit he and his partner had created, the safety kit that was at the core of the business. It was a fairly simple kit containing essential safety provisions that were critical on an oil rig. It was easy to source the products contained in the kit. My driver had been focused on using the safety kit as an entry point for the training that he was offering, but I thought that the safety kit itself was the more valuable and marketable business idea.

For days after that taxi ride, I was thinking about those safety kits. I was excited. I knew exactly how to market those safety kits—we could place ads in journals and publications that targeted directors and managers of offshore oil rigs. We would describe and promote the product, and the mail orders would flow in. I was confident that I had connected the dots between the unsuccessful safety training business my driver had attempted and a much bigger and more lucrative product sale.

That idea, sparked by a ride in a taxi, became my very first entrepreneurial venture.

It was not a success.

I've spent some time thinking about this first business, peeling back the onion layers to reflect honestly and critically. I remember the energy and enthusiasm I felt, the conviction that this idea had the potential to become extremely profitable. I failed to notice any red flags; it was inconceivable to me that this business could fail.

What I didn't know then, what I know now, is that enthusiasm and a great idea are only the beginning steps of a successful business. It's what follows that is even more important.

Your business must withstand the kind of scrutiny provided by the strategic framework I'll share in the chapters that follow. You'll need to rely on more than instinct to ensure that the opportunity is real, the customers can be targeted... and that you have the financing in place to support your plans.

These reality checks are vital, and I encourage you to do the work, answer the questions, research your market, and position your venture for success. I don't want to put up roadblocks. Quite the opposite. I want to equip you with the knowledge so that you'll be able to identify potential obstacles before they appear and be prepared to navigate around them. I intend to be transparent about what hasn't worked for me and identify the times when I've simply been lucky. I have to continuously remind myself of what I've learned and redirect myself back to the framework that helps point out those obstacles before it's too late.

I promised to share my stories—the successes and setbacks—so that you can learn from my experience. And I'll start with this very first entrepreneurial effort.

I launched the business. I funded my startup for two months.

And then I ran out of money.

I was a university student. I didn't have the money to start a business. But more importantly, I allowed myself to be carried away by the idea without scrutinizing it strategically. A great idea matters, but at the heart of every truly successful entrepreneurial venture is a problem that is identified—and solved.

I'll return to this question throughout the book: ***What problem are you solving?*** With every new business, it's important to ask this question. I never asked that question with my safety kit idea. In fact, it wasn't even my idea. It was a good idea, but a good idea that belonged to the taxi driver. It had been successful for a little while when he and his partner first started the business, and I thought that I could take a piece of their idea and make it mine, increasing the success in the process.

> My first mistake was failing to clearly identify the problem that I was solving. The second was that I didn't do my homework. My goals were not informed by data and an understanding of the market potential. In order to measure success, I needed to know the actual market size I was targeting. How many customers were there for the safety kit? Would success involve selling tens of these kits, or millions?

And finally, as I mentioned earlier, I hadn't prepared adequately for the financing of my business. I hadn't identified the amount of cash I'd need to fund the business or achieve sustainability, let alone become profitable.

Start With Questions

In this book, I'll encourage you to ask questions. I'll share my experiences—the questions I've learned to ask that have proved vital to ensuring that a business is positioned for success. I'll urge you not to be passive but to actively engage in critical thinking. I'll coach you to look beyond the potential of your idea to identify the challenges. Too often, we look at business plans in a black-and-white model. Either an idea is good or it's bad. But I think the business world is far more nuanced. An idea can be good, and yet it may not be right for you; the market potential may not generate the profit you want, or the investment may be greater than you're able to fund.

That's why the strategic framework in this book will be a valuable tool. It will equip you to move beyond judging whether an idea has merit to analyzing whether a specific entrepreneurial venture makes sense for you.

Not every business you launch will be successful. But with each experience, you gain understanding and knowledge and are better equipped for the next venture.

Whether you're leading a family business in a new direction or launching a startup, you can't predict each phase of your business's life cycle. There will be setbacks and new opportunities. But with a solid framework—a strategic framework—you'll be able to prepare, pivot, and position your business for a better outcome.

In the chapters ahead, I'll share the step-by-step process of building a framework that has worked for me, one that you can tailor so that it makes sense for your unique goals. We'll discuss where to begin, creating a strategy that is realistic, clear, and actionable. We'll break down the fundamentals of market share and industry dynamics. I'll share advice from business experts and strategic thinkers on how to identify and target your ideal customer. We'll analyze the key financial markers that will support profitability and growth and then assess how to build a team that is committed, skilled, and dedicated to delivering results.

There's incredible support for entrepreneurs right now across the world, especially in those countries that top the list: Germany, United States, Japan, United Kingdom, China, South Korea, Canada, Singapore, United Arab Emirates, and Saudi Arabia. I believe in this effort and welcome the fresh energy and enthusiasm that's sparking innovative thinking in a wide range of industries. I've had many conversations with aspiring entrepreneurs who want to be successful, and who want to launch businesses that can thrive and contribute in a meaningful way. I welcome these conversations and am inspired by the young people who are dreaming big.

This book is my way of sharing what I've learned so that you can do even more. As a fellow entrepreneur who is still learning and adapting, my goal is to equip you with the tools and strategy that I've found valuable. My hope is that you'll find some nuggets, some techniques, in these chapters that will help you successfully launch and grow your business.

If you have a great idea, which is supported by a solid plan that answers the questions laid down in this book, I invite you to connect with me to pitch your venture. I will be happy to act as both an advisor and as a possible investor in your startup. The details on how to connect with me are provided at the end of the book.

Chapter One

What's The Problem You're Trying to Solve?

"The essence of strategy is choosing what not to do."

—MICHAEL PORTER

I'VE BEEN FORTUNATE TO benefit from the examples and mentorship of several extraordinarily successful businesspeople. One of them is my father.

My father launched his business, Arabian Hala Company, in 1977 in Riyadh. This was in the days before the internet, before any of the research tools that are available to entrepreneurs today ... even before faxing.

My father's strategy depended on a clear approach: identifying a need that was not being met in the market. In the late 1970s, Saudi Arabia was going through some wonderful changes. The discovery of oil had been of great benefit, and prices were increasing. Construction was booming. There was an influx of consultants and contractors from construction companies and oil companies, all of whom needed cars to navigate the Kingdom.

My father had spent time in California, and while he was there, he rented a car. Rental cars were not then common in Saudi Arabia, but my father recognized that the demand was there. The market potential was strong. He simply needed to supply the product that would meet that demand.

My father's goal was specific. He wanted to be the leading supplier of rental cars in the country. He had spent time studying companies that were successfully doing this in other countries. He researched and confirmed that there was significant potential for rental cars if he could provide reliable, quality vehicles.

Hala Rent-a-Car launched with a modest twenty-seven vehicles. As the business grew and became more successful, he was able to add more cars. Eventually, he was awarded the exclusive Avis franchise, and today the company has a fleet of more than ten thousand vehicles and employs more than three thousand people.

What's interesting to me about my father's example is how he developed an initial strategy and then allowed the strategy to evolve over time, setting new goals and identifying a framework to achieve them. He leveraged the success of the rental car business to expand into new ventures—into manufacturing, supply chain services, freight and transport, and courier services.

I mentioned that the company he created employs more than three thousand people. I've been fortunate to observe the value of his strategic thinking up close, as one of those employees. I started working in the rental car business when I started at university. You may think that because I was the owner's son, I started in a position of significant responsibility, maybe as an executive running an important division. No, my father placed me as a sweeper in one of the workshops.

There is tremendous value in working in a business from the ground up. You can really find out what is going on in the company. You see how customers are treated. You observe the managers who are good and those who are not. You hear and see everything.

There is tremendous value in working in a business from the ground up.

Of course, because I was the owner's son, I wasn't treated like a typical sweeper by my colleagues. But the funny thing is that my age was an even bigger liability. Being young was seen as a weakness.

At this entry-level position, after about six or seven months, I noticed that some of the managers were misusing their position. I told my father, and he investigated further, discovering that they were embezzling from the company. It was a mess, and several people were fired. It was a valuable lesson that a wise entrepreneur learns as much as he can about what's happening at all levels of the business, and for me, it provided an opportunity to see how strategic thinking can depend on the ability to look at your business from top to bottom, identify problems, and learn how to respond effectively.

Solve a Problem

The business my father launched and grew is a great illustration of this chapter's theme. The best strategic framework for a business depends on a key first step: creating a strong and sustainable strategy. You may have a wonderful idea, a strong team, and significant resources. But without strategy—one that is clear and communicated consistently—your business will struggle to succeed.

I've spent a lot of time studying different aspects of strategy, looking for the concepts that resonate with me. I think that it's helpful to engage in these kinds of exercises, to explore and learn from the very best minds and find ideas that make sense for you and your business.

In this book, I want to share my experiences, but I also want to share what I've learned. Michael Porter is one of the scholars whose writing on economics and business strategy has been especially impactful for me. You'll find more about him and his theories in chapter 3, but I appreciate his quote at the start of this chapter.

"The essence of strategy is choosing what not to do." —
MICHAEL PORTER

Strategy depends on your ability to make choices. In some cases, it requires you to consciously make certain choices and actively stop making other choices. The purpose of these strategic choices is to deliver something that will solve a problem for a person or group of people in a way that is economically sustainable. Building your strategy will require you to say yes to some things and no to others.

It can be a bit overwhelming to connect the dots between your decision to launch a business and the need to build a strategy. So let me start by asking you a few questions:

- What is your inspiration?

- What is your end goal?

- What is your dream?

- What does success look like for you?

In order to create a strategic map to guide you to your goal or target, it's helpful to begin with a lot of clarity about where you want to go.

Perhaps you're struggling to find a great cup of coffee on your daily commute. You've noticed that there are no good coffee shops in your neighborhood, and you decide to open one yourself.

Successful entrepreneurs identify a problem and then find a solution, but your strategy will help you move beyond problem-solving to actually building a viable business. Let's take a look at your goals for your coffee shop. Do you want to offer coffee that's fast and convenient? Or create a communal space that is inviting, one where people will gather to talk while they sip coffee? Is your goal to open a single local shop or become the next Starbucks?

You can begin to see that different answers to these questions will produce very different strategies. In a sense, you start by forming a clear picture of what success represents in your mind and then work backward.

I do want to point out that the answers you supply now, at the start of your entrepreneurial journey, are not fixed in stone. They will become clearer as you gather more information and begin to form your strategic framework. You may deviate from your original answers—and that's perfectly fine! The end goal that you ultimately achieve may not be what you had envisioned when you began. I don't want you to feel pressured to identify a single path to success. There may be different paths to the success you are seeking, but the strategic framework you develop when you launch your business will be based on this important step of visioning—setting some specific goals that you can then work to achieve with your framework.

Perhaps your goal is to have a specific income, enough to pay your bills, your mortgage, or your rent. Maybe you plan to hire others to work with you and will need income to cover multiple salaries. This is where you start to shape your strategy.

With this information, you'll be able to determine whether your goals are possible. Is there a big enough market in the neighborhood for you to sell enough coffee? Do many people want the kind of coffee experience you plan to offer?

Strategic planning requires you to start with the end in mind.

What does success look like for you?

What will be a "win"?

Look into the future to get a clear picture of where you want to end up, and then return firmly to the present because:

- you need to then take a careful look at the idea you have,

- the plan you intend to implement, and

- determine if the market exists for you to achieve this dream.

If a market exists, you can move forward confidently. But if it doesn't, you must go back and find out what needs to be changed for you to achieve your goal—or if it is even possible.

There are so many business theories that are fluffy. Strategy isn't like that. It's tangible. You can build it like a Lego set.

Applied Learning

My father is just one of the mentors who've shaped my thinking about business and strategy. My participation in the Young Presidents' Organization (YPO) introduced me to another important influence whose ideas on strategy I want to share with you: Dr. Rebecca Homkes.

Let me take a step back and tell you a bit about the context in which I first encountered Dr. Homkes. YPO is a global organization of young executives who are committed to becoming better leaders and better people. It's a fantastic community, and I was incredibly fortunate to join it in 2009 when I was twenty-nine years old. You have the opportunity to network with other executives, learn from their examples, and share ideas and strategies.

To be honest, this impressive group can be a bit intimidating. Different countries produce different leaders, and leadership styles that work well in one setting may not always be a good fit in another. These networking opportunities have shown me that some leaders can be more aggressive in their management styles and may choose to focus much more intently on growing and expanding into new markets. That kind of peer pressure—being among leaders who are taking decisive actions to build up their businesses—can be intense.

I made the mistake early on of thinking that maybe I needed to be a different leader—more like those who were the first to share their successes in our meetings. I was more aggressive and demanding of my employees. I tried it for about two weeks.

I was absolutely miserable. I didn't want to go into the office.

And I'm sure that my employees didn't want me there either.

That's why it's helpful for me to make sure that I do what I discussed earlier in this chapter: keep focused on a strategy that is based on the goals and end targets I've set to avoid being distracted or tempted by others' strategies.

I've had to build a lot of knowledge and understanding the hard way. After earning my MBA, I came back to Saudi Arabia with a significant quantity of self-confidence. I thought, "I have an engineering degree. I have an MBA. I'm ready to rule the world. Give me any company, any startup, and I can take it to a billion dollars at least."

I remember one moment in my young and foolish past very clearly. I was sitting on a black leather sofa in my brother's office in the family business. This business is structured as a holding company with several independent subsidiaries, including the rent-a-car division, logistics, import and tire distribution, and finally an under-performing automotive retail company that handled the sale of new and used cars and a network of automotive repair shops.

It was that last entity that intrigued me. I told my brother, "We have this struggling company. I know I don't have a background in the automotive sector. I know I don't know how to sell cars. But it will be challenging for you to find a new CEO to replace the current one, who is underperforming. The company is losing money. Put me in there as interim CEO for at least six months while you identify a good CEO, and we'll take it from there."

I didn't stop to think carefully about strategy, my goals, and the strategic framework. I just went into that company determined to turn it around.

I struggled. And kept on struggling from one issue to another, to another, and to yet another. It was one of the lowest points of my life. My education and MBA training went out the window because nothing I had learned about economic theory really fit into the problems I was encountering day after day.

The company I was trying to turn around was focused on selling new cars and also operating vehicle service centers. I had heard of the SEMA automotive trade show held every year in Las Vegas. It's an event where they highlight the latest product and custom-vehicle trends, and different suppliers of automotive spare parts exhibit. In desperation, I decided to attend the event and see if I could learn anything that would help turn the business around, any trends or developments that could be brought back to Saudi Arabia.

One of the great benefits of the YPO network is the opportunity to speak with other members. While I was in Las Vegas at the SEMA show, I scheduled a call with a YPO member named Vinny Lo Civero. We were supposed to speak for fifteen minutes; we ended up talking for well over an hour.

Vinny recommended an Active Learning program that YPO was offering on business strategy, part of an Applied Learning series of intensive training opportunities. Vinny warned me, "This is not a typical academic program like the programs offered by Harvard or London Business School. And you may not like what you find out.

What Vinny explained was that the program would provide a way to address, specifically and in detail, the problems our business was experiencing. You come in not on your own but with your executive team. You go through the discussions, the learning, and the planning, as a team, and then you go back to your company and implement what you've learned together as a team.

I was willing to try anything, so I assembled my executive team, and we flew to London. Within the first thirty minutes, my sales manager spoke up and said, "I know what our problem is. We don't have a strategy." It was absolutely shocking to me. But then I realized that he was right. After this revelation and a detailed discussion, we continued to work through the program. The training on strategy was so impactful that by the end of the program, I knew what I needed to do. I went back to Saudi Arabia and closed the struggling company's new car sales division.

Vinny was right. I didn't like what I learned during the strategy training. But it was the kind of knowledge that has helped me learn how to avoid mistakes and make better business decisions. And I want to share it with you here.

Rebecca Homkes On Strategy

Dr. Rebecca Homkes is the director of the YPO's Applied Learning program. She is also a teaching fellow at the London Business School's Department of Strategy and Entrepreneurship and one of the leading writers on high-growth strategy.

As you build your strategic framework, Dr. Homkes is a valuable resource whose writing on strategic execution will ensure that your framework is as robust as possible. A good starting point is an article that she coauthored for *Harvard Business Review*: "Why Strategy Execution Unravels—and What to Do about It".[1]

Dr. Homkes is a frequent speaker on strategy execution; a quick summary of her insights is available in a *Corporater* interview on YouTube (https://www.youtube.com/watch?v=9NT5o-gCJ-Y).

Rebecca walked our team through her five questions of strategy. These are five questions that you'll want to carefully consider and even more carefully answer. I've found them to be central to the ability to build a successful framework for a business:

1. What's the situation?

2. Where will we compete?

3. How will we succeed?

4. What's going to stop us?

5. So what should we do?

The first two questions are, in some ways, the most important and the ones that will reveal a great deal. These questions equip you to dig deeper, to

---

1. Donald Sull et al., "Why Strategy Execution Unravels—and What to Do about It," Harvard Business Review, March 2015, https://hbr.org/2015/03/why-strategy-execution-unravelsand-what-to-do-about-it

think about how to understand critical points. What is the situation you are entering? What is the market size? What's happening in the industry? What are the trends, and who are the leading players (if any)? And how will you compete?

These were the questions that prompted my sales manager to state, during that training in London, that we didn't have a strategy. If we did have a strategy, it was a "me too" strategy, based on copying the successful model of others. We didn't have a competitive advantage. There was nothing unique about what we were offering.

It was a terrible discovery and one that we could have avoided by asking these questions at the beginning, as I'm encouraging you to do. I didn't want to quit, but this wasn't simply a matter of not wanting to keep going because the circumstances were challenging. Rebecca's training and questions forced me to recognize that there was no path forward with the existing business model.

The best thing you can do is ask these questions as part of the earliest stages of launching your business. The Active Learning program will always have a special place in my heart because it taught me to ask those questions and to begin to build the confidence to walk away from choices and opportunities that aren't sustainable.

How to Build Your Strategy

Rebecca's questions are a great place to start as you begin to build a strategy for your business. In order to answer these questions, you're going to need to invest time and effort in research to learn everything you can about your market. Learn what is happening in the industry in which your business will be operating. Gather data about your potential customers and your potential competition.

Rebecca also recommends assessing what you can influence going forward. I love this; it's so helpful to stop and think about what is true today and what might change in the future.

Let's go back to the coffee shop example we discussed at the start of this chapter. What is the problem you're trying to solve? Perhaps it's that you've had too many cups of bad coffee and want to supply a better alternative.

Your second step is to identify how many people in your neighborhood may want to have the same problem solved. How many others—your potential customers—are looking for a better cup of coffee? If you are the only person complaining about coffee, you don't have a business. If you find enough people who are looking for great coffee, you have a viable opportunity and a path forward.

I find it helpful to take a step back and consider exactly why I'm starting a business. Is it ego? Is it simply that I want to say that I've started something that's now worth billions of dollars? Am I trying to be the next Jeff Bezos, or is there an actual problem that I'm going to solve for other people?

With the coffee shop, consider what will create your competitive advantage. What specifically will make your coffee good—or even great? Perhaps you will roast the beans for six hours instead of three. Perhaps you will single-source your beans from Colombia rather than having a combination of beans. Avoid the temptation to look at other coffee shops and focus on replicating their branding, their seating, or their coffee machines. Instead, think about what you will do differently.

You don't have to be the next Starbucks if that's not your goal. You don't have to copy someone else's success. But answering these questions means that you need to spend time thinking about your market, your community, and how you can make things better for other people.

The lessons I learned about prioritizing strategy have helped me make smarter decisions for the company I lead, SAC (Specialized Automotive Company) Motors. Our supply chain is so unique that it can't be replicated. Most of the workshops in Saudi Arabia are mom-and-pop stores—a single owner and a single location. We have three branches in the country, so we are already three times the size of our competition. When we buy spare parts, we buy them in bulk. Those significant purchases mean that we can expect a discount on our orders. Other subsidiaries of our family business, including the Avis Rent-a-Car division, also use spare parts. This means that if we combine the buying power of SAC Motors and the Avis division together, we'll be purchasing even larger quantities, and negotiating significant price discounts.

If one of our subsidiary companies needs spare parts, our supplier will prioritize that order, simply because we are such a significant customer. We will get the parts we need.

That is a success—a success that cannot be replicated easily by any of our competitors. And so, as we develop a strategy, we will want to use that competitive advantage as a launching point. We can leverage our supply chain advantage to build out future business ventures.

The Strategic No

Another important lesson I've learned from Rebecca is the importance of saying no. It connects to the Michael Porter quote at the start of this chapter; strategy depends on being wise in choosing what to say yes to and which opportunities to say no to. Sometimes it's not saying no to an opportunity—it's saying no to a customer.

I work in the automotive sector; collision repair is a big part of what we do. Because of that, I want our business to be known as the collision repair experts—that's our niche, and we want to grow in a way that continues to develop and cement that reputation.

As part of this collision repair service, our employees have the expertise to do tire balancing and change tires. They can do the necessary mechanical and electrical repairs on the car. They can repair body damage. They can paint the vehicle.

Now, suppose my team comes to me and says, "Our customers have been asking us to change the oil in their cars. Look at how much money we will make if we start to offer oil changes."

These are the kinds of situations where it's critical to step back and consider Rebecca's strategy questions. My goal is for our company to be known as "the collision repair expert". We can offer this service competitively because of our supply chain.

If we decide to expand our business to include oil and filter changes strictly because customers are requesting it and we can make more money, then we are no longer focusing on our reputation as the company customers go to when they need collision repair. Our competitive advantage in accessing low-cost spare parts does not translate to routine car maintenance; we must charge full price for oil changes.

Next, I think about why a noncustomer might come to me for an oil change, to make sure that I'm not missing an opportunity to reach a new customer segment. My research shows that customers' decisions about who they will hire to perform an oil change on their car depend very heavily on convenience. Your location matters in order to be competitive in this service. That means that, if I do decide to move into the oil change market, I may need to consider an investment in new locations, which will change the cost structure and may dilute profits.

I've learned that saying no to opportunities, to customers, and even to employees becomes much easier with a strategy in place, one that identifies what you want to accomplish and what makes you uniquely positioned to succeed.

The Strategic Framework Every Entrepreneur Shall Follow

Dr. Homkes has written about the importance of a three-year cycle for strategy for mature companies and a one-year cycle for new startups. These three-year or one-year increments are a helpful way to design your plan for your business. They support a framework that enables you to answer the strategic questions I've shared throughout this book.

But it also prompts you to revisit those questions as your business grows, as the market shifts, and as new opportunities arise.

The Strategic Framework:

1. What's the problem you're trying to solve?

2. What is the market size?

3. Is this industry sustainable going forward??

4. Who is your ideal customer—and what specific value are you offering them?

5. How is the cash flowing?

6. Who are the people you need on your team?

7. What Are The Potential Pitfalls to Success?

8. How Will You Execute The Strategy?

Answering these questions requires research and data. I have developed a Google Sheets format that works very well for me. It forces me to input critical data, things like the hiring statistics (the salaries that will need to be paid for three years) and the revenue streams to create a specific profit and loss document. With that kind of data, it's much easier to compare your dream with the harsh reality of the numbers to determine whether or not you will be generating the profit you need to make.

If the answer is no, you don't need to immediately give up. But you do need to reconsider each of these questions again. Each business has a different character and different things you need to focus on to achieve success. With data in hand, it's possible to examine your assumptions and identify areas you may need to change or alter.

If your profits are too low—or nonexistent—identify where the losses are coming from. Is it from a lack of revenue? Too many employees? Too many high salaries? Consider where you might make changes. Do those changes need to take place in the rent you are paying, in production, or in sales? As you narrow in on these answers, continue to ask questions. If you need to increase sales, how many salespeople will you need to add to get the right revenue, or what type of training will you need to provide to your current sales team to achieve those sales?

One of the things it took me some time to realize is that a profit and loss statement is a wonderful gauge. Really, it's a scoreboard. At the end of the game, you look at the scoreboard. But you also check it throughout the game to see how well you are playing. As you make those periodic checks, you will discover that you may need to make changes—to the team members, to revenue, to marketing—and then check your progress and see if the score has improved.

You'll discover that you won't be able to say yes to everything. But a strategic framework will help you choose the right yes for you and for your organization.

I have made a lot of mistakes. One thing I've learned is that the successes I've been lucky enough to be part of have come from very simple businesses—the businesses where you understand what you can do and you do it well and provide good service and good products.

I was in Portugal recently, and one of the things I noticed was that there were many great restaurants there. The chefs put true passion into their food. In a restaurant, they are cooking the same meal at least twenty times a night. They may have been making that meal, with those ingredients, for three months. These were restaurants that generally had a fairly small menu, maybe with four different options. It made me think. Imagine in your business that you only have four projects, and your focus is simply on continuously improving them. It's likely that you will start to achieve an extraordinary quality, one that might take a competitor years to catch up with. If your focus is on what you want to deliver—and delivering it at a high level of consistent excellence—you will be successful.

It's much harder to deliver that same quality, that same excellence, with forty dishes. It's much better not to be everything for everyone but instead to be something for someone. Focus on what you do well, and then do it even better.

After a particularly wonderful meal, I spoke with the chef to give him my compliments. He was able to tell me a story about every single piece of food that we ate. Each small part of that meal mattered to him.

A strategic framework will ensure that you focus on what matters to you and your business. It will enable you to bring consistency—and passion—to the product you're delivering. And that's what success requires.

Part I

Understanding Market Dynamics

Chapter Two
What Is the Market Size?

"We've had three big ideas at Amazon that we've stuck with for eighteen years, and they're the reason we're successful: Put the customer first. Invent. And be patient."

—JEFF BEZOS

IN THE PREVIOUS CHAPTER, we began the process of thinking strategically about your business. An entrepreneurial venture often starts by identifying a problem you want to solve. But to make that transition from problem-solving to operating a profitable business, you need to determine who else has the same problem and what they would pay for a solution. That requires you to identify the potential market share.

Gathering data and thoughtfully researching market share is absolutely critical. Too often, a problem that is bothering you, something that you are facing and needs a solution to, proves to be simply an individual problem. It's specific to you; no other buyers are interested.

Let me give you an example. I have found it very difficult to find a good barber in Riyadh, Saudi Arabia. This is something that frustrates me. It's a massive problem for me. It became such a frustration to me that I finally thought, "You know what? If I have this issue, other people must have the same problem. I'm going to start my own barber shop. I'll hire the barbers that I think are really good and expand the search to find really good barbers globally. I'll build up a business. I may even be able to franchise it around the country."

I was convinced that I had found a new business opportunity. I went and did some research to determine how much this barber shop would cost to set up, how much I would need to spend, and where I might identify the resources I would need. I did a lot of research to find a solution to my problem.

But then I discovered that it was, in fact, my specific problem. I started asking my friends about barbershops and good barbers in order to find barbers I might hire, and all of them quickly referred me to the barbers they used and the shops they patronized. I had so many referrals! It was clear that what I thought was a massive problem was, in fact, specific only to me.

My research also uncovered the realities of the market, and it was much different than I had expected. Barber shops are only a small subset of the men's grooming market in the region. Another small subset is hairstyling. The biggest portion of the men's grooming market in the Kingdom is in beard-care products. You have beard cleansing products, beard masks, waxes, gels... all of those beard-care products form the biggest share of the men's grooming market.

I was forced to recognize that my problem was very small and very specific, although it felt significant to me. More importantly, the solution I had devised would barely generate enough revenue to cover its costs. It would never generate the massive return I had envisioned.

What I've learned is that every market has specific nuances that are critical to an understanding of the market size and market share. There's only one way to discover the information you need to determine whether or not your business idea is sustainable, and that is through research.

Every market has specific nuances that are critical to an understanding of the market size and market share.

You need to ask questions—of potential customers and of people who have already been in that industry.

In the barbershop example, I recognized a problem: I was having trouble finding a good barber. My first step should have been to ask other people if I was correct—if this problem actually existed. Once I did that, what I heard was, "No, not at all. I can give you the name of a good barber. I can give you the name of ten good barbers.

But what if my friends had agreed with me that they, too, were struggling to find a good barber? If I spoke to ten friends and at least five confirmed that my problem was also their problem, I would want to find out more.

Triangulation

Triangulation is a technique researchers use to analyze data in a holistic and comprehensive way. It is a strategy that you can employ to develop a clearer and fuller picture of your market, enhance the validity of any assumptions you've made, and cross-check results.

Triangulation depends on gathering data from different sources and using different methods. I recommend using it as part of the process of building your strategic framework and forming a more detailed picture of market share.

Think of the three points of a triangle. Your goal will be to gather data from three different sources. This should give you a clearer picture of the potential market for your product or service, or possibly the minimum and maximum size.

Your first data point will come when you buy an industry report, giving you critical data about market size and industry trends. A good place to start is with a Google search. There are quite a few firms that provide industry reports. If you are serious about your business, it is worth the investment to buy one. They can cost around $2,000, but this is a valuable tool to truly understand the nuances of your potential market. You want to be fully familiar with the factors that are impacting it. You want to know how big it is and what the potential size could be for your product or service. That's the information that will tell you whether the potential market size is acceptable for you as an entrepreneur. It's not a matter of whether it's small or large; it's more important for you to calculate whether the potential return for your investment is something that excites you and positions you to achieve your goals.

A decent industry report will give you the market size for your industry as well as the possible subsets. Check the industry report to find out the sources of the data that are being used to determine precisely where the data is coming from. Verifying the data source is important when you're consulting multiple reports; too often, the data all comes from the same place, so you may think that you're gathering information from more than one source, and yet it is all stemming from the same data bank. That's dangerous when you are trying to create a broader picture of the industry you want to enter.

Once you've assessed these industry reports to build a high-level view of your industry, your next step is to gather information about other businesses that are providing the kind of service or product you're planning to create. Consider the barber shop example I noted earlier; you need to go to a barber shop and get friendly with the barber and ask some questions. This step is a way to verify the numbers you've developed. How much do they charge for haircuts? Do they charge for additional services? How much money do they make from selling grooming products, and is that a big contribution to the revenue structure?

The same research can help you understand cost structures. How much does this barber get paid? Is it a profit-sharing relationship with other barbers or with the business owner? This kind of information is especially critical if you are an outsider, like I was, with no previous experience in the industry except as a customer.

You want to find out, for example, whether twenty dollars for a haircut and a shave is an average ticket size for that barbershop. Of course, you don't go to just one barber shop; you go to several. You get a clear picture of the range of prices, the range of services, and the potential demand for your business.

The third point of the triangle is the most difficult. This is where you really need to do the legwork. It involves drilling down into the specifics of each piece of data, every number that is integral to your business plan. Using the barber shop example, you need to find out exactly how many barber shops exist in the city (or the country) and how many licenses are granted each year, and then start to understand and create alignment among all of the different data you've gathered and the assumptions you've made for your potential business.

Let's say that I've learned that there are about three thousand barber shops in Saudi Arabia. My research has shown that one barber shop should have about twenty clients a day and that each barber shop has two barbers. I need to use these separate sources of data to create a full picture of the potential market size and then use that data to check my assumptions. Will I be able to attract the clients I need, at the prices I will be able to charge, to generate the profit I am expecting?

Your goal is to be able to enter your data into a spreadsheet and make sure that your assumptions are correct. Make sure that you know how many clients you need, and how much each client will need to pay, in order to generate the kind of profit that makes you excited and that makes sense.

Focus on Numbers, NOT Feelings

It's important to think critically about the data you uncover in your research. Let me share an example. Logistics is vital for all businesses but especially for those operating in manufacturing. It involves managing the flow of products or resources from their point of origin to the point where they reach the customer; this includes their acquisition, their storage, and their movement or transportation to their final destination. It involves a successful supply chain, one in which products and services move smoothly and efficiently from beginning to end.

Most countries measure logistics based on a country's GDP. Those numbers have led me astray more than once. If I look at a Saudi market with a GDP of over 800 billion, and the logistics numbers suggest that the potential market share is more than 3 percent of that 800 billion, that's a huge market.

But then you start to dig deeper. And you discover that the Saudi GDP includes oil tankers as part of the logistics. Saudi Arabia is the largest exporter of oil in the world. That's going to skew the logistics data.

Suppose that your intent is to transport or warehouse freight or some other piece of the logistics industry. If you look at that 800 billion number for Saudi GDP and discover that logistics is more than 3 percent of it, you may incorrectly interpret that to mean that your logistics business will be able to generate that kind of profit. But if your intent is to develop a transportation business or warehousing or freight forwarding or some other subset of the logistics industry, you must be diligent and look further to identify precisely what share of the logistics market your specific service represents. Warehousing, for example, may be much, much smaller than the 3 percent you thought it would be. These are the nuances you want to understand before you launch your business.

The purpose of this is to eliminate the emotion around your entrepreneurial decision-making. You don't want to rely on your gut or your senses to conclude that this business will be potentially massive. You can use triangulation and research to determine how realistic your assumptions are and to decide whether or not the venture makes sense for you.

I say "for you" because ultimately, you are the only one who can determine your deal breakers, the results, or scenarios where the data will tell you to shelve your business idea. I don't think there is a "correct market size." It goes back to your willingness to take risks and how lucrative the market needs to be to get you excited.

If I'm going to do something, I want it to be big. I'm always looking to scale the businesses I run, so my decision-making will depend on whether a business I start can be franchised or expanded beyond the borders of Saudi Arabia. The research I do needs to show potential to scale up the businesses I start in order for me to be enthusiastic or passionate about a new venture.

But this may not be true for you. Your business may be a nonprofit or a service venture that simply needs to break even. It's a matter of making sure that you are content with the return that you can realistically expect.

Question Your Assumptions

One of the most important aspects of researching market potential is to know what you don't know. It's tempting to get caught up in the energy of a new opportunity and to think you've asked the right questions and done the necessary homework only to discover that your assumptions were wrong.

I said it in the introduction, but it's worth repeating here: I've learned more from my failures than my successes, and one of my goals in this book is to share what I've learned to hopefully equip you to avoid the same mistakes. So now I'll share one example of a time when I discovered that my assumptions about market size were incorrect.

In the late 1990s and early 2000s, there were multiple terrorist attacks in Saudi Arabia. It was a frightening and terrible time, with many bombings and violent incidents. At some point in the early 2000s, when there was a lot of concern about the ongoing threat from terrorism, together with my father and brother, we were about to launch a security company that would sell bomb-detection equipment and other equipment to detect the presence of large quantities of gunpowder. The company would offer a product that could enable others to identify and protect against threats from car bombings or people carrying bombs or other weapons that would cause harm.

We were excited about this opportunity to protect people and to sell a product that was so desperately needed in the Kingdom. We knew that people would buy it, and our immediate reaction was "Let's go ahead and do this."

So that's what we did. We launched the company. We signed an agreement to source the equipment from the UK, and then we spent a lot of money trying to sell that equipment.

The business failed. It failed for several different reasons. First, it failed because we didn't understand the security business. Frankly, we didn't ask the right questions and dig deep into our research. We knew that there was an urgent need for this product—there was a problem that we knew how to solve. But we didn't invest the time and effort to thoroughly explore the industry we were entering.

We knew that there was a large market in the Kingdom for security, but we didn't break it down into its specific sectors. What I now know is that we should have determined what percentage of the security market was for personal security, such as security guards, and what percentage was for security equipment. We then should have explored other types of equipment—things like metal detectors and concrete barriers—and determined which types of security protection had the greater commercial potential. We should have identified our customers more thoroughly to understand precisely how many people were going to buy our equipment. Would there be mandates from the government to have them installed, or would we be dependent on an individual risk assessment?

That's where we failed. We knew that there were bombings. There was a clear security threat. There was a need for protection from terrorist attacks. We were presented with an opportunity to help provide that protection and we moved forward.

A second issue was that we didn't thoroughly research the company from which we were buying the equipment. It emerged much later that the technology they were using didn't actually deliver the results that had been promised.

Would I go into this business today? No, I would not. The market quickly became saturated with suppliers of different security products. Our assumptions that there was a strong need for our product were false. In a crowded market, you must be able to identify what it is that makes your product unique. In the case of the security equipment, the answer was absolutely nothing. We didn't have a superior product. We didn't have a superior sales team. We didn't have a superior marketing strategy. We didn't have a superior anything at all.

In addition, we didn't know the industry. We didn't understand its key drivers or the nuances that would shape demand. We didn't have a strategy to win.

Beware of Baboon Dust

Let's spend a few minutes exploring market share, because as you look into a potential market, you may discover that the space is crowded and challenging. That doesn't mean that you should abandon your venture; it just means that you need to test your assumptions and ensure that you are comfortable with the potential risks you may be undertaking. We operate an online car auction website as one of our businesses, selling cars for our group of companies via online sales. A B2B business. We were challenged with the possibility of expanding this business to a B2C product and launching it to the mass public.

We started to explore the market using the steps outlined in this chapter. We did the research, determining market share, average pricing, and all the necessary information. It's a huge market. And it's very lucrative.

But what we discovered, as we started digging deeper, is that quite a few other companies have already started similar ventures. Several are multi-nationals that have entered the Saudi market. There are also two or three locals who launched a few years ago and are now accelerating their pace.

Part of my assessment, as I think about this business, is assessing the amount of risk I'm willing to undertake for the business. Does it make sense to do it on our own—launch the company, build the necessary infrastructure, and deal with the challenges of competitors? Or should we partner with those competitors, identify one who is likely to be the most successful, and approach them about a joint venture? We could provide them with the vehicles in exchange for shares in the company or some other arrangement. Since the market is competitive, does it make sense to enter the market and compete with these other players or merge and join forces with one of the more established competitors?

Part of this research process involves carefully studying the competition. Look at their marketing, study their sales, and learn as much as you can about how they are performing. Are they delivering on what they are promising? Are they as good as they say they are?

I have looked at a beautiful marketing campaign from one of these competitors and become incredibly discouraged. I have to tell myself, "Hold on, Husam. You don't know. You don't know how successful they are. This might be just baboon dust."

Baboon dust is this fantastic phrase that I first heard from a friend of mine from South Africa. It refers to the fact that when you approach a baboon and it wants to protect itself, its hair sticks up. And then the baboon starts to kick sand in the air to make itself look bigger than it actually is.

That's why I caution you to beware of baboon dust when you're looking into potential competitors in your market. Those competitors may just be trying to make themselves look bigger than they actually are.

Talk to Advisors

I've learned not to rely on my own instincts or even just the data when it comes to making critical decisions about entering a market. Once you've done your research, created Google spreadsheets, and tested your assumptions, sit down with some trusted advisors and talk through your plans.

I'm lucky to have a few good advisors who will give valuable feedback when I'm considering a new venture. My brother is one of them.

My recommendation is that you also collect trusted advisors. Identify those people whose business sense you trust, some of whom have experience starting and launching successful ventures. Ask for an hour of their time. Show them your numbers and the research you've done. And then ask them whether or not it seems like a good idea. Invite their honest feedback.

You may discover that you need to do more research. You may learn that you will need more revenue to cover your expenses. Be open to learning as much as you can.

Usually, people have blind spots. It's difficult to see the complete picture when you only have one perspective, and it's quite important to see as many perspectives as possible before actually jumping into a business. That's why I like consulting advisors.

Your team of advisors will be most helpful if it includes people with different skill sets. You may wish to consult an advisor who has successfully launched and grown a business, another who is successful in finance, and another who is successful in sales. You may want to consult an expert in technology if your business will depend on e-commerce or automation. Their expertise will enable you to ask specific questions; for example, you can show an advisor who works in finance your numbers and ask them to make sure that they make sense.

Your advisors will likely come back to you with more questions than answers. That's exactly what you want. Those questions will inspire you to sit down and think more about your process. They will also push your boundaries and drive you to work a bit harder! People who have been successful know which questions to ask.

If you're in the B2B space, consult an expert who could be a potential customer. Show them a prototype or talk through the service you're proposing, discuss your planned pricing, and ask them if they're interested.

In the end, there are no guarantees. There will always be more questions you can answer and more research you can do.

You will never have 100 percent certainty. So strive for 80 percent. The point of researching your market is to ensure that you don't go into a business with your blinders on and only discover that it wasn't successful after you've lost money and the business is shuttered.

Your research should create comfort around risk, giving you the knowledge to move slowly and purposefully into a market, not simply jumping into the deep end of shark-infested waters. It's about building confidence that you have what you need to achieve your goals.

Too many entrepreneurs focus on the thrill of an idea, on the opportunity to solve problems. That piece is important, but I know a lot of failed businesses that started with 80 percent gut instinct and 20 percent data. My suggestion is to shift that ratio. Keep the spark and the innovation, but you also need a lot of data and research to prove that your business is viable and to understand every nuance of the industry you are entering.

Identify the problem you want to fix. Make sure that your organization is the right one to solve the problem. Do the research to test your assumptions, and consult advisors to make sure that your plan makes sense.

Getting Ready to Talk to an Advisor: An advisor is someone who has experience in building companies like yours. A startup advisor can be an invaluable asset to help you structure your company, raise funding or replicate your business solutions for profitable growth. If you want somebody to help you steer your venture, your prospective advisor shall not only have the knowledge and skills you lack, but also a real interest in your startup idea. A valuable advisor helps compensate for your weaknesses. Also, an advisor might have connections and contacts with people that you don't know. This means your advisor can open doors to prospective service providers, investors, partners, and key executive employees that you wouldn't otherwise have access to.

As a thank you token for reading this book and for applying the learning found in its pages (by taking action), I invite you to schedule an advisory session with me. The details of how to reach out to me will be provided towards the end of the book. I strongly recommend you read all the book and have all of your questions prepared to make the most out of this call with me. If you'd like to stand out of the crowd, I recommend you present your business plan or investors pitch deck on our call. You never know, I could

have an equal interest and passion for
your starup idea that I may invest in
it and become your advisor to make it
the success it deserves to be.

With a strategy in place and a clear picture of your market, your next step is
to prepare for the potential barriers you may encounter when launching a
business. In the next chapter, we'll discuss how you can continue to build
your strategic framework through an exploration of the key concepts of
industry dynamics.

Chapter Three
Is This Industry Sustainable Going Forward?

"Strategy is about setting yourself apart from the competition. It's not a matter of being better at what you do—it's a matter of being different at what you do."

—MICHAEL PORTER

AS YOU BEGIN to build your strategic framework, you'll want to spend time assessing and studying industry dynamics.

Recently, I had a conversation with a small business owner and began to talk to them about the importance of industry dynamics. This individual held up their hand.

"Husam," they said, "can you use real-world language? Just tell me what I should be doing."

I laughed. "Know what business you're going into," I said, "and recognize how the industry is changing."

That conversation was a helpful reminder to me of the times that I've struggled to sift through the writings and recommendations of business experts. Their information is helpful, but the language that's used can be off-putting or hard to decipher. I've been challenged in the same way as the owner with whom I spoke. I want to understand what those experts are saying—and, perhaps more importantly, be able to identify how their research and insights apply to the work I'm doing and the work I want to do.

Let me start by providing an explanation from John Mullins, whose book *The New Business Road Test* shares helpful recommendations for entrepreneurs before they launch a new venture. Mullins explains the critical difference between market dynamics and industry dynamics (the latter is what I'll be talking about in this chapter). Mullins notes that markets are essentially a group of current or potential customers—the buyers. An industry is the sellers—the people or companies that are offering goods and services. That means that the market is the who, the people who will become your customers. Industry dynamics focuses on something different, helping you to understand how you will compete.

In the next few chapters, I'll share what I've learned from several thought leaders whose strategic insights have made a significant difference for me professionally and personally. In the process, I'll try to keep it simple and help you understand what you need to be doing to implement their insights in your entrepreneurial ventures.

Getting Serious About Strategy

I enjoy reading business books, and my favorite books—the ones I pick up first—are those that focus on strategy. I've read somewhere that there are more than one hundred different business strategy models, from SWOT analysis to blue ocean strategy. I believe that if you take the time to truly understand this kind of strategic thinking about business, it's possible to achieve something that is dramatically different from your competition.

Michael Porter is considered one of the leading authors of business strategy. He's an economist, a researcher, and a professor at Harvard Business School. His writing encourages you to think about some core questions that every entrepreneur should be asking. Why are certain companies more profitable than their competitors? Why are certain industries more profitable than others? These are questions that have serious implications for anyone thinking about launching a business.

Porter has written thousands of pages on business strategy. His books *Competitive Strategy* and *Competitive Advantage* have been in print for more than three decades and are still taught as essential texts in MBA programs.

That's where I first encountered Michael Porter's writing—in my MBA program. I wish that I could tell you that I fully understood and quickly began to apply all of his insights, but that would not be honest. Porter's writing is dense and challenging. But as management expert Joan Magretta notes, "If you are serious about strategy, Porter's work is the foundation."[1]

I quote Joan Magretta here because it was her writing that helped me begin to decipher the key insights of Porter. I had read two of Porter's books and couldn't understand them. Then I read Magretta's book *Understanding Michael Porter*, and it was transformative. She explained Porter's frameworks using case studies and real-world examples. Her discussion of

---

1. Joan Magretta, Understanding Michael Porter (Boston: Harvard Business Press, 2012).

Porter's most famous framework, the one focusing on the five forces, was especially helpful.

Once I had read Magretta, I could return to Porter's writing with a much clearer sense of how it impacted me and my businesses. For example, Porter says, "Strategy is about making choices, trade-offs; it's about deliberately choosing to be different."

This is a core element of business success, don't you agree? Deliberately choosing to be different requires you to know the business you're going into and identify the competitive advantage you can provide. You need to understand every aspect of the industry, need to become informed on the trends that have shaped it and those that will impact it in the future. You must be able to recognize your potential competitors and be very clear on what you are bringing to the industry that will be unique.

> **Deliberately choosing to be different requires you to know the business you're going into and identify the competitive advantage you can provide.**

I'll share many of Porter's quotes in this book, and I could spend several chapters on his strategic thinking, but for now, I want to focus on Porter's five forces framework. This framework will help you assess your competition strategically by learning about your industry and clarifying how and where you can have the most impact in it. I like Porter's five forces framework because it helps fill in the assumptions you have of an industry. It equips you to truly understand what is going on, how you might fail, and, most importantly, what you can do to stop, avoid, or mitigate risks.

I've learned to think differently about competition as a result of this framework. I had thought of competition as taking place between two opposing teams or individuals, with a winner and a loser. The winner, I thought, was the one whose product or service was the best. But what I've learned from Michael Porter's writing is that successfully competing in business isn't dependent on who is arbitrarily judged to be better. It's whoever is the most profitable.

Getting Started With Michael Porter

Michael Porter has been described as the founder of the modern business strategy field. His writing can be challenging, but his insights have been invaluable to me. If you're serious about launching a business and want to think and prepare strategically, Michael Porter's writing will equip you with critical knowledge. He's written nineteen books and hundreds of articles, case studies, and research papers, so you have plenty to choose from, but I recommend starting with one or more of these:

On Competition, Updated and Expanded Edition by Michael Porter, published in 2008, gathers more than a dozen of Porter's most impactful articles published in the Harvard Business Review. It includes his original paper on the five forces framework that I discuss in this chapter as well as detailed research that reflects his thinking on strategic CEO leadership. This is a good place to begin to explore Porter's writing on competition and value creation.

Competitive Strategy: Techniques for Analyzing Industries and Competitors by Michael Porter: This book is required reading in many of the world's leading MBA programs. In it, Porter discusses how three factors—focus, cost, and differentiation— can impact a business's ability to position itself for success.

Competitive Advantage: Creating and Sustaining Superior Performance by Michael Porter: This builds on Porter's Competitive Strategy by further exploring the criticality of understanding your environment to then identify how to strengthen and more effectively position your business.

The Five Forces

Thinking about profitability is an important starting point in your assessment of industry dynamics. It's a matter of fully understanding the industry in which you plan to compete and using this understanding to create a value proposition—the who, the what, and the how that will generate profitability. Porter's five forces framework has helped me clarify this process by equipping me to identify the tradeoffs that may be needed to achieve a competitive advantage, and I encourage you to consider how his framework could be adapted to your venture.

Porter has identified five separate forces that impact your ability to operate profitably. Profit isn't simply determined by your competition—by what other businesses are charging. Profit is also shaped by your customers and what they are willing to pay. It's impacted by vendors and how much they will charge for materials or services. Your profits may suffer if new competitors enter the market or if new products are introduced that could compete with yours.

These are Porter's five forces:

1. Rivalry among existing competitors,

2. Bargaining power of buyers,

3. Bargaining power of suppliers,

4. The threat of substitute products or services, and

5. The threat of new entrants.

The above five forces are all important but not necessarily equal in weight. Depending on your industry, one or another of these forces may be more powerful and, as a result, more likely to impact prices, costs, or both.

Porter first introduced this framework in an article published in *Harvard Business Review* in 1979. He explained the strategic importance of the framework in a way that demonstrates why I'm highlighting its value so many decades later: "A company strategist who understands that competition extends well beyond existing rivals will detect wider competitive threats and be better equipped to address them. At the same time, thinking comprehensively about an industry's structure can uncover opportunities, differences in customers, suppliers, substitutes, potential entrants, and rivals that can become the basis for distinct strategies yielding superior performance."[2]

This framework has helped me assess industry dynamics to determine if a business makes sense for me. It has also helped me measure a business's performance to understand what's working and what needs to change.

---

2. Michael E. Porter, "The Five Competitive Forces that Shape Strategy," Harvard Business Review, January 1, 2008.

You may want to try using Porter's five forces in asking—and answering—important strategic questions:

- *Existing competitors:* Who will be the direct competitors for my business or service, and what impact will they have on my ability to be successful? How can I differentiate my business to eliminate this threat?

- *Customer power:* What actions must I take to attract—and keep—customers? What additional services should I offer to maintain customer loyalty?

- *Supplier power:* What impact will vendor pricing have on my ability to be profitable? Do I need to identify alternative sources/suppliers or expand the network of vendors I'm using to respond to the impact of price increases or product shortages?

- *New entrants:* How should I prepare for new entrants into my market? What investments should I undertake to make the market less attractive to new competitors?

- *Substitutions:* Which new products or services might lure away my customers? How can I offer better value to reduce or eliminate this threat?

These questions have helped me recognize that Porter's five forces are not fixed and static. They can be responded to in a way that ensures profitability.

They also can be important ways to identify and respond to new trends. Understanding industry dynamics is more than simply knowing the industry you're entering today; it's also recognizing how the industry will change in the future.

The Automotive Example

I find Porter's writing quite helpful in building out a strategic framework to determine whether an opportunity makes sense—in essence, to confirm that it is as good a deal as it seems. Let me share an example from an industry I know well: the automotive industry.

The automotive industry has different sectors, and understanding each of them is key. When I consider the automotive industry's dynamics, I need to break down the industry into its pieces. There are new and used sales for cars and new and used sales for trucks. The industry also includes spare parts, servicing of cars and trucks, collision repair, automotive finance, manufacturing, and insurance businesses. All of these sectors form part of the automotive industry.

When I'm looking at a business in the automotive industry, I will note that the industry might be a $10 billion segment in which we could compete. But it's critical to recognize that 80 to 85 percent of that segment is in vehicle sales, and if you are not launching in that area, you're left with something very small. You may have a huge appetite when you jump in, but your potential profitability is considerably smaller than you thought.

This is why I encourage you to spend time thinking about industry dynamics. You must understand exactly which segment you're going into. With that knowledge, you must go a bit further. You must take action to recognize what is changing.

Let's go back to the automotive industry. I'm very focused on the collision repair aspect. The biggest changes I'm looking at in the industry that will impact this collision repair aspect are the potential introduction of new safety features and self-driving vehicles. I need to examine their impact in the short and long run.

What does this mean? It means that I must ask strategic questions. I must think about whether these disruptions are likely to happen in the next year or two, or in fifteen years. How long will it be before people are less likely to have accidents?

Another change that will impact my repair business is the fact that newer cars are made out of aluminum. That changes how you repair cars because welding or fixing aluminum is a very different skill set than doing so with steel-built cars.

These are the factors that you need to think about as you prepare to enter an industry, as you make decisions designed to grow a business... even as you seek to understand where your business is profitable and where it is not. You need to be prepared to ask probing questions about the environment of your industry, studying trends to recognize what might change and what will impact you going forward.

If you're looking at launching a venture in a new industry and wondering where to get started, I have a simple recommendation. Start with a Google search. The information that's available today is vastly different than what I had access to when I started twenty years ago. Research, read, and not just one source. Verify with multiple credible sources to make sure that the information you're accessing and the trends that are being projected are correct. That initial research will become the foundation you'll use to ask questions and test your hypothesis—the steps we talked about in the previous chapter.

Let's look again at my example of the automotive sector. Perhaps you do the research, and you discover that 80 percent of your sector is automotive sales, but the remaining 20 percent is still substantial enough for a very targeted business that you're planning to launch. What's next?

The purpose of doing your homework, of engaging in the research at the start, is to ground you. You don't want to be shocked or surprised at the potential market for your service. You don't need to build an infrastructure for a $10 billion industry when it's only a $2 billion industry. I've seen it happen before where an aspiring entrepreneur looked only at the big picture, at the $10 billion industry potential, and assumed that meant there were $10 billion in potential sales leads waiting for them. Then they go out, try to close deals, and get discouraged.

"What's wrong with me?" they wonder. "There's a $10 billion industry out there and I can't even tap into it."

Entrepreneurs are given to self-doubt, especially in the early stages of launching their venture. The frameworks I've used are a great way to eliminate at least some of that self-doubt with data and detailed industry specifics.

I'm using these strategies even as I write this book! I'm recommending them because they are frameworks that continue to impact my decision-making. Just recently, I was exploring the possibility of expanding our online car auction business. We have a prototype—we've sold about two thousand cars online in a live auction. It's tempting to think we'll sell even more if we expand that business, but I wanted to explore the industry dynamics using Porter's five forces and ask other strategic questions about the potential profitability of that segment of the used car business.

I like to use Google Sheets, but you can use whatever format makes sense for you. I started with the existing data—the cars we've sold, the profit we earned, and other relevant costs and expenses, as well as my projections of the market size and the share of that market I anticipate taking. Then I played with the numbers to see if it made sense to launch an online car auction website. How much of an investment am I considering? How much will I need to achieve to break even? How much to earn a profit?

I didn't need to rely on gut instinct or be influenced by my enthusiasm for this venture. The data was clear. I could see that we would be losing money for the first eighteen months. It would take five years before we began to earn a significant profit. The data showed that there were potential threats from other new entrants into the industry and that it would be difficult to take any steps to build a repeat business in the short term. This showed me that it would be a more strategic and ultimately more profitable decision to partner up either with one of the existing players in the industry or with one of my competitors who was planning to enter the industry than launch something on my own.

This should be a plan you consult often as you launch and build your business to make sure that you are not deviating in a significant way from your assumptions and projections. If you are, you must take a careful look at where your results or expenses are different to understand how to correct and shift. Is there something that you failed to recognize? Porter's five forces framework can be helpful here to identify potential changes in your business's environment that may require you to rethink your initial assumptions.

Barriers to Entry

Porter's framework has helped me think about a key aspect of industry dynamics: barriers to entry. Simply defined, barriers to entry are those obstacles or factors that make it difficult for a new business to enter an industry. They might be things like high startup costs or existing brand loyalty. Identifying the barriers to entry must be part of your research into industry dynamics so that you can prepare and respond before you launch a new business.

The barriers to entry will be unique depending on the business you choose to launch. Right now, there are many Saudi entrepreneurs thinking about opening a food truck business. It's a popular venture, and for good reason—people always want quick, convenient food options. It will probably cost about $15,000 to launch that food truck business. How many people can afford that? As I said, it's a popular route to entrepreneurship right now, and the cost is one reason—quite a few people are able to raise the $15,000 initial cost. That means the cost barrier to entry is relatively low. Your competition will likely be higher, and your potential profit likely less.

Instead, suppose that you decide to open a centralized bakery that sells baked goods to all of the food trucks in the city. Of course, a fixed building with the equipment that a bakery requires will have higher initial costs; it will be more expensive to start a business like that, probably ten times as expensive as a food truck business. That's a higher barrier to entry, so it might be a smarter option for your business because there will be fewer competitors able to raise the funds.

There are many barriers to entry that you'll need to identify, not simply for your own preparation but also to recognize the industry dynamics and the forces that may shape your ability to operate profitably. There may be local regulations in place that limit the number of specific kinds of businesses that can operate within a certain community. If you're the first to start that business, great! You'll know that your competition will be significantly reduced—or eliminated—because of existing regulations. There are other regulations beyond zoning that can create those barriers to entry. Manpower can be another barrier—there may be a limited number of people with the skills you'll need.

Survey Your Landscape

I've learned to enjoy the process of understanding industry dynamics for any business I'm considering. But this is a lesson I had to learn the hard way.

One of the first companies I was asked to scale up was a supply chain service. It included warehousing, freight forwarding, customs clearance, and logistics. When I first went in, I'll admit to being young and a bit arrogant. I approached every client meeting as if I was the authority. My first brochure was fifty pages long—yes, fifty pages! I put everything into it that I could about logistics and included plenty of claims about how we were the best.

The good news is that I can laugh now at my younger self. I was so concerned with demonstrating our value that I focused too much on talking about our business and too little on surveying the competitive landscape. I didn't spend time identifying our competition. I didn't research which parts of the supply chain segment they were in and where they were not—and why.

I tried to position the business as a consulting service, an implementing service, and a third-party provider all at the same time. It didn't make sense, I recognize now because we certainly couldn't offer an impartial consulting service; we would always be biased about our own services. My attitude did not help attract clients.

Finally, I was negotiating with a big client after multiple rejections. We prepared a memorandum of understanding (MOU). Because the client was not a fluent English speaker, the MOU was prepared in both English and Arabic. The Arabic translation of the original English text ("the company owns the intellectual property") was not clear, and our wonderful client read the MOU to mean that he was lacking in intellect rather than relinquishing claims of intellectual property. Of course, he was understandably offended. He walked away from the deal and did not return. It took months before I could fully understand what had happened. We had insulted a potential client simply by using the wrong language.

I share this story to explain how easy it is to make a mistake by not doing your homework, failing to read every document, not taking the time to survey your environment, recognizing what your customers need and what the competition is doing, and then making sure that you deliver. It took me quite some time to understand how to scale this business more effectively, given the industry dynamics. Ultimately, I recognized that we didn't need to do more. We needed to do less, to simplify our service offerings, but do it better, more cost-effectively, and in language that made sense to our customers.

Final Thoughts

I'm sharing my stories and strategies throughout this book, but it's important for you to recognize that you should use these as a springboard to create a framework that makes sense for you and your business. Your industry will have unique barriers to entry. Your goals will be uniquely yours, as will the markers that will show that you are on the right path.

Your industry will have unique barriers to entry. Your goals will be uniquely yours, as will the markers that will show that you are on the right path.

I love competition. Whenever I think about launching a new business, I always start with the point of view that I can solve the problem I've identified and that I'm going to make millions of dollars because no one else can do exactly what our business will be able to do. I think most entrepreneurs start from that position of idea plus confidence.

But I continue to use Porter's five forces as my business scales, studying the competition, the barriers to entry, the impact of new products, and customer loyalty. I was recently studying one of our competitors for our car repair shop division. They are a big venture; they have mega-workshops, one of which is as large as three of ours. But we were receiving a lot of business in that market, and I wanted to know why. What were we doing well? What should we focus on and build on? Because of their size, I knew that it wasn't capacity. So what?

I discovered that our success depended on two factors. One was the price. They were more expensive than we were, probably because of the cost of maintaining a larger infrastructure. The second was time to completion.

On average, it took them twenty-one days to repair a car. We were able to repair the car in nine days.

These are huge competitive advantages, which matter to both the customer and the insurance companies that pay for the repairs and may need to supply replacement vehicles while a car is in the shop. But as we thought about the industry dynamics and the competitive landscape, we recognized that price was a less strategic factor for promotion purposes. Our large competitor might be able, because of their size and deep pockets, to engage in a price war. And a new competitor might enter the industry and undercut us on price.

However, our quick and efficient turnaround time, with a quality repair job delivered rapidly, was something that would be difficult to match. That's what we identified as our clear competitive advantage, and that's what we chose to promote on our website. And we continue to promote that today.

It's easy to get lost in economic theory and forget that, in the end, it comes down to one key question for any entrepreneur: What is my strength? Or in other words, What am I good at?

Your business's ultimate success won't depend on being the only one in the industry. It won't matter if you're bigger or if you have fancier equipment or better technology or more people.

Profitability will be the measure of your business's success. It's critical to recognize what you do well and what will make that thing different from anything else available. Identifying the industry dynamics will help you survey the landscape to create that competitive advantage.

Part II
Offering Value to Your Ideal Customer

Chapter Four

Who is Your Ideal Customer—and What Specific Value Are You Offering Them?

"Most successful entrepreneurs are comfortable with being uncomfortable most of the time."

—REBECCA HOMKES

I APPRECIATE THE QUOTE from Rebecca Homkes that starts this chapter. Rebecca is a teaching fellow at the London Business School's Department of Strategy and Entrepreneurship. She also consults with CEOs and executive teams of global businesses, sharing her expertise in creating and executing strategies that support growth.

Rebecca is a thought leader whose recommendations made a significant difference in one of my business ventures, as I shared earlier in this book. She has also shaped my thinking about building a more strategic approach to all aspects of my business, including my customers. As an entrepreneur, I've found customer management to be challenging.

In the last chapter, we talked about the power of the customer as one of Porter's five forces. It seems obvious, of course. If a customer decides they love your product or service, you have the potential to succeed. If they hate it ... well, you need customers to have a profitable business.

The biggest challenge when it comes to the power of the customer is that what they value is not a static element. It will change depending on the economy, their needs and resources, and sometimes even on the weather. In my businesses, quality is important—the quality of service. But service is an area that matters far less to customers when there is a downturn in the economy. In those situations, the price suddenly becomes far more important to most customers. Cheaper is often more important to those customers than faster.

As an entrepreneur, you may be examining this question of pricing and customer expectations. May I share a bit of advice? There will always be pressure to lower your price, but I'm not convinced that this is the best arena for any business to focus on its competition. Unless being thrifty is going to be your company's competitive advantage— unless what you want to be known for is being the cheapest alternative—then I suggest not going in with low prices, especially not if your thought is to keep prices low at the beginning and then raise them later. It's very difficult to raise prices if the only story you've told to your customers is that you are the cheapest.

Instead, the story I tell my customers is one that focuses on how good we are. I remind my customers with our marketing and sales campaigns, with every interaction, that we are different because we are better. I invite them to compare us to our competitors because I am confident that we will win those comparisons. It's important to me to deliver products and services that I'm proud of. I don't want my salespeople to spend a lot of time negotiating every service or every repair. We set a price that's fair and competitive in the market. We aren't the most expensive, and we aren't the cheapest. But then, we tell the story behind that price—we explain what the customer has received in return.

When the car is repaired and the bill is presented, our team reminds them that we finished repairing the car in four days when the industry average is twenty-one days. We explain where we managed to save on the spare parts we used because we received a discount from our supplier and passed some of those savings on to the customer. We point out the extra services we provided. If a car comes in to repair a rear bumper and we see some additional scratches, we will polish them out and then tell the customer that this was done at no additional cost while the car was in the shop.

We want the customers to know that their business matters to us. It's important that we show how we are better. The secret to good customer service isn't always to be outstanding; it's to be better than they may have expected.

Customer service experiences are typically rated on a scale from 1 to 10, and most businesses, if customers take the time to rate them, receive a 5. That shows that those customers received essentially what they expected in the time they prepared for and at the price they expected to pay. An average experience.

I don't want my business to be average, so we try to deliver something that's a little unexpected. That extra polishing of scratches, for example, or cutting a day off our turnaround time. But the key is to make sure that the customer knows what you did. I'm trying to earn that 10 in customer service, of course, but even a 6 or 7 is fantastic. If you are a little bit better than your competition, your customers will return and recommend you to others.

When we return the car to the customer, our team tells that story. They go through what has been done, they explain the extra service that's been provided, and we ask our customers to rate us on Google if they're satisfied with our work. That last step is so important, and I drill it into our team again and again—ask for that rating. When you're looking for a new service provider or searching for a specific product, you'll either ask someone you know or you'll search on Google. If most of the businesses have a three- or four-star rating and one of them has a five-star rating, that's the one you'll choose. I want those customers, so we work hard to earn every one of those stars.

I realize that when you're starting a business, there's a lot to focus on. Most of the entrepreneurs I talk to want to just jump in and get started. When it comes to customer strategy, they intend to learn as they go. But this is an expensive path.

I'm recommending these key pieces in your strategy framework not because I want you to overanalyze each part of the process. But entrepreneurship is a marathon, not a sprint. It's important to train and prepare in an intentional and methodical way and to put in place systems that will be sustainable and will enable you not only to operate profitably but also to scale and grow. And in order to scale and grow, you need a strong and flexible customer strategy.

Who is Your Customer?

Steve Jobs famously described Apple's DNA as being centered around its reputation as a "consumer company—for that individual customer who's voting thumbs up or thumbs down." He recognized Apple's importance as an innovator, and as a market leader, but was conscious of ensuring that, in the end, Apple was making products that people were eager to buy.

The only way to do this is by knowing your customer, by being able to describe them in detail and identify how your product or service will make their life better. What problem do they have that you will solve? What will you do to earn not just their money but also their loyalty?

Rebecca Homkes explains that a customer is not always simply one person. Instead, customer decision-making may involve up to three people or groups of people: influencers, buyers, and end users. The influencer, as their name suggests, helps to determine whether or not your product or business will be selected. The buyer is the one who ultimately pays for the service. The end user is the one who actually benefits from your product, as they will consume it, engage with it, or use it in some way. What Rebecca showed me—what I now encourage you to do—is to think carefully about my customers in these terms and then create a value proposition for each.

Suppose that you are thinking about launching a coffee shop in your neighborhood. You've studied the industry from a big-picture perspective, analyzed potential competitors, identified what will differentiate you from them, and determined where to source your beans and the other products you'll offer. Next, you need to build a specific customer strategy.

When you think about a customer, you probably think of one individual—the person who will actually walk into your shop and purchase a cup of coffee. Using Rebecca's framework, however, we can start to recognize that the buyer is only one potential type of customer. Let's suppose that your coffee shop offers not only coffee but milkshakes. On a typical morning, I want a cup of coffee. As I'm getting ready to leave, my three kids ask to accompany me because they want milkshakes. My wife recommends your shop because your business is known for its healthy ingredients.

Suddenly, there are three types of individuals shaping the decision to patronize your shop. I am the buyer—I'll be paying for all four drinks. My kids are the end users of the milkshakes; they will drink them but not pay the bill. My wife is the influencer; she's the one who specifically directed us to your shop because of its reputation for using healthier ingredients than some of the other shops that serve coffee and milkshakes.

In this example, the influencer (my wife) is visible and vocal to my kids and me, but remember—the shop owner may never have known what prompted the four of us to enter their shop to buy coffee and milkshakes. Influencers are often invisible in this way, and their impact may be negative as well as positive.

Imagine that you are promoting a new app to a corporate client. You make your pitch before a room of executives; you hit all of the key points and leave feeling very confident. You didn't hear any objections or negative comments. But what you don't know is that after the meeting ended, one of the executives spoke to another in the corridor and began to point out a long list of potential problems, problems that you could have responded to had the questions been raised in the meeting. That executive will not be the one purchasing your app, nor will they be the user. But they have an impact on the company's technology decision-making. Ultimately, the company decides not to buy your app, and it's because of the impact of that influencer.

Of course, these roles can overlap. To go back to the coffee shop example, someone might walk into your shop, buy the coffee, and drink it. They are then the buyer and the end user. But when your customer is a B2B customer—if, for example, you're selling a product or service to another company or business—they may have a procurement department that is responsible for all purchases the company makes, but the service or product you provide will be used in a different department by a different set of individuals.

This is why it's critical to build a strategy and a value statement specifically directed to each of these three categories of customers. You need to know who is paying for your service, who is consuming or using your service, and who will impact any decision-making between your service and that of your competitors.

For example, the end user's need (the focus of their value proposition) might be speed and efficiency. The buyer's need might be price or efficiency. And the influencer might be impacted by something altogether different—perhaps how the product or service you're offering can be integrated into the company's overall growth or operations.

I dedicate a lot of time to building a strategy around these three categories in my businesses. In my repair shops, say someone has an accident and brings in their car. That customer is the end user. What matters to them—their value proposition—is that the car will be returned to them in the same or better shape than before they had the accident.

The buyer is that individual's insurance company. The insurance company will pay for the car to be repaired. What is important to them is that the repairs are made at a lower price. When we create a value proposition for the insurance company—the buyer—we focus on the fact that we will deliver quality at a reasonable price much more quickly, eliminating the need for the insurance company to pay for a replacement vehicle or a rental car. The car will be repaired correctly, so it will be reliable and less likely to quickly break down again, requiring another repair.

The influencer in this case may be the CEO of the insurance company. (It could also be the financial manager or even the sales manager.) That individual wants satisfied customers, claims paid efficiently, and no follow-up claims or complaints. Our value proposition for that influencer is our efficient turnaround time, our ability to access the parts that are needed for repairs at a reduced cost, and our reports of satisfied customers.

The Hidden Customer

I've focused on strategy in this chapter, but equally important is the hard work of talking to each of your potential customers. When you launch your coffee shop, for example, you may not know that there is a strong demand for milkshakes. You may think that customers want pastries with their coffee and then discover that your business is suffering because customers want sandwiches instead. These are sometimes described as "complementors"—in fact, complementors are often considered to be a sixth force in Michael Porter's framework! Complementors are something extra—services or products that complement or add value to, what's already being offered. They're more valuable together than individually. Where would the iPhone be without the iTunes store and Apple's App Store?

So how do you identify what your customers want? The solution is straightforward: you need to ask. You need to talk with the people who you anticipate becoming your customers and find out what they need. But it's more than simply asking. Suppose you talk to three people, and they all agree that they want a coffee shop and that the most important thing to them is price. What might be hidden is the fact that there is also a demand for milkshakes, and the milkshakes must be healthy. Or many of the customers feel that it's important that the coffee they drink is fair trade or grown and packaged in certain regions of the world. All of those pieces of information are hidden. So how do you find out these hidden customers and invisible demands?

I talked earlier about assumptions, and this is where Rebecca's five questions can help you avoid the trap of not asking the right people the right questions. It's not enough to simply ask a potential buyer if they want a coffee shop in their neighborhood. You need to ask about the experience. Do your customers want to grab a cup of coffee quickly on their way to work, or do they want more of a social experience, where they lounge, do some work, or read a book? If it's a social experience, what impact will that have on the music playing, the types of seating you offer, and even the size of the cups? If it's workers on the go, stopping to get coffee and immediately carrying it out, perhaps you don't need to offer expensive seating or invest in a large footprint for your shop.

It's critical to recognize who your customer is and who they aren't, and which services you'll provide and which you won't.

This isn't a one-time effort. I periodically revisit and reverify these three customer groups for my businesses, because they can and do change over time. One of the biggest mistakes companies make is that they don't realize that their customers are changing and their needs are changing with them. A value proposition that you've created for a specific customer group may no longer make sense in three or five years' time. Disruptive technology, changing demographics, changing behaviors, changing tastes... these all can cause a shift and require a new strategy. I recommend revisiting your customer groups once a year to make sure that your value propositions are correct and your assumptions are still true.

It happened recently to us. One of the companies I've been working on is launching a software to manage trucks. We identified our buyers, end users, and influencers, breaking them down by industry. It seemed that we had a solid business plan in place. But over the course of a few months, we learned that the software was appealing more to customers with lower profit margins. Quality was less important than price. We had been focusing on creating software to manage trucks with high-end refrigerants, and we realized that the software was more attractive to material companies with trucks shipping items that didn't need to be refrigerated; they wanted low-cost and efficient delivery. It shifted our approach to the software business—it was still a viable venture, but we recognized that our assumptions about our customers needed to be modified.

These assumptions can change the whole dynamic of the business and its financials as well. We'll talk about those more in the next chapter.

But each question you ask should circle back to the idea that prompted you to start the business in the first place: ***What is the problem, and how will I solve it?*** As your business grows, as you identify new problems to solve, you may discover that you need to create value propositions for new buyers and be prepared for some of the buyers you appealed to at the beginning to no longer patronize your business.

When it comes to my coffee, I generally like speed and quality. I want a large cup of good coffee served to me quickly. I then take it to my car and drink it on the way to the office.

I used to love Dunkin' Donuts coffee for this reason. There were very few options, maybe cream or sugar. You could get a donut with your coffee, of course, but the transaction was very quick. You didn't need to wait for a barista to prepare a fancy hot beverage. You got your coffee and your donut and were on your way in about two minutes. Then Dunkin' Donuts expanded its menu. It started offering bagels that needed to be toasted with a variety of toppings. They added foam-based drinks that took longer to prepare. Suddenly, I'm waiting longer and longer in line while customers in front of me have special breakfast sandwiches and double-shot lattes prepared.

From a business standpoint, this probably made sense to the Dunkin' Donuts management. Customers wanted more specialty espresso drinks and breakfast sandwiches. There was an opportunity to respond to a problem and to increase their profits. But I no longer stop at Dunkin' because my need—good-quality coffee served quickly—was no longer being met.

No business can be everything to every customer. The goal should always be to focus on what you do well and your competitive advantage and make decisions informed by that understanding.

The furniture maker IKEA is another great example. Their value proposition is centered around offering good-quality furniture at reasonable prices. But they are able to deliver those two factors because the furniture is supplied in parts that the customer must then assemble. In focusing on that core differentiator, IKEA recognizes that it is turning away customers who want premade furniture, but they have built a profitable business while being able to say no to customers who want ready-made pieces.

Ask How

Many entrepreneurs make the mistake of identifying a problem, looking at the competition, and thinking "I can do better." They believe that they can deliver a product or service faster or cheaper without understanding the underlying business.

They fail to ask how. How will they achieve their goal? How will they do it better or faster?

Author and Harvard Business School professor Cynthia Montgomery warns of what she calls the "myth of the super-manager." These are leaders who are so confident in their own abilities that they don't recognize that there are factors beyond their control. "Their most common mistake," Montgomery writes, "is to underestimate the limitations on opportunities in many industries."[1]

It's an unfortunate danger for entrepreneurs. They get an MBA from a top university and believe that they can launch or fix any business because of their education and skills. What they need to do, what every entrepreneur must do, is take the time to ask how. If they're competing on price, where is that advantage coming from? From the rental agreement, they've negotiated for their location? From a supplier advantage? What are the details, and what about it will be difficult for a competitor to replicate?

As an entrepreneur, you may find it helpful to recognize your own customer experiences to help you identify and more thoughtfully shape your own customer strategy. Think about a time when you interacted with a

---

1. Cynthia Montgomery, "The Myth of the Super-Manager," Management Issues (Management-Is-s sues.com), accessed September 8, 2022, https://www.management-issues.com/opinion/6507/the-myth-of-the-super-manager/.

company or business and felt confident that they understood your needs and were shaping their business to respond to them.

For me (and I recognize that it's a bit cliché to say it) an example is Apple. I'm a big fan of their products. I feel that they understand me when it comes to my techiness. When I go from a Zoom call on my iPad to a phone call on my iPhone, my AirPods switch seamlessly from one to the other. When I talk to Siri, I have the sense of becoming Tony Stark talking to Jarvis in Iron Man. Apple successfully makes me feel tech-savvy and integrates products in a way that makes sense to me without requiring me to overthink any of the products I'm using.

I'm not typically someone with a lot of brand loyalty, but there is another area where I feel that a company understands me as a customer. That company is Porsche. Because of my engineering background, I appreciate the beautiful engineering that goes into their cars. I love how the car's shape has stayed nearly the same for the past seventy years, but they just keep getting better. It appeals to my sense of perfectionism. I love the Porsches I've owned; I even name them. And in case you are wondering, my current Porsche is named Lili.

I'm also a loyal customer of the Marriott hotel chain, based solely on their app. If that app didn't exist, I wouldn't stay there as frequently as I do. But that app enables a wonderful booking functionality. It easily tracks how many points you have with them, and how many days you've stayed. The user experience is fantastic. But there's another element of that app that is especially appealing to me. I don't love having long conversations with people in order to complete a transaction. Efficiency is important. The app actually helps me with that. Not long ago, I landed at the Los Angeles airport, and the app sent me a prompt asking if I wanted to check into the hotel in Newport Beach where I was staying. When I confirmed, it notified me that my electronic room key would be ready shortly. I had packages that I had ordered from Amazon; they were delivered to the hotel and placed in my room, something I arranged through messaging within the app. When I walked into the hotel, I didn't need to go to the front desk to check in; I went straight to my room and used my phone to unlock the door, and the packages were in my room waiting for me. It's like having your own butler who takes care of everything; there's just a bit of magic to it. Not every experience has been perfect, but that sense of magic, of your needs being fully understood, is what most customers are looking for.

I share these experiences as a way to illustrate that even the same customer will have different needs and require different value propositions, depending on the product or service you are offering. The same individual may need efficiency, high-end design, or tech-enabled integration, depending on the product or service.

I've been lucky enough to participate in a program in Saudi Arabia called the 2030 Leaders. It's a group of leaders who are committed to carrying out the Kingdom's Vision 2030, discussing how best to solve economic and social problems in the Kingdom and implement innovative transformations to create positive change. The goal has been to identify one thousand of these leaders who will then move the Kingdom toward these new opportunities.

We've had several fascinating discussions and opportunities for learning, and much of the conversation has centered on artificial intelligence (AI) and how it can contribute to improving our quality of life. I like the idea of centering AI not as a replacement for human beings but as an addition—as a way to improve and facilitate more authentic moments of human connection.

You can leverage technology and data to create a business plan that makes sense on paper, but in the end, it comes down to people. Your business's success will depend on your ability to recognize the very real people who will be your customers and build your business based on how you can make their lives better.

Part III

The Resources That Will Set You Up for Success

Chapter Five
How is the Cash Flowing?

"I've never gone into business to make money. Every Virgin product and service has been made into a reality to make a positive difference in people's lives. And by focusing on the happiness of our customers, we have been able to build a successful group of companies."

—RICHARD BRANSON

THE MOST SUCCESSFUL entrepreneurs I've known have followed the message in Richard Branson's quote at the start of this chapter. Their focus has been less on the money they might make and more on the problems they can solve.

When I talk about the importance of understanding your finances as you build your strategy framework, I'm talking about something very specific and concrete, centered less around your projected revenue—although that matters—and more on the data you build that will touch on all aspects of your business's financial health from day one. Most companies don't fail because they're not profitable. They fail because they run out of cash.

It reminds me of the famous quote by Alan Miltz: "Revenue is vanity, profit is sanity, and cash is king." Understanding cash flow will be critical for your success. You'll need data to recognize how long it will take for your investments (whether in products or inventory or other expenses) to be converted into cash, something known as the cash conversion cycle.

As you build a strategic framework for your business, your framework will create a picture of your business. That picture must be cohesive. Your financial data must reflect your strategic framework. Your financials need to be reflected in the products you choose to purchase, the suppliers you use, the location you select, and the people you choose to hire. As an entrepreneur, you must examine both your strategy and your financial data and make sure that both of them are reflecting the same picture.

> **As you build a strategic framework for your business, your framework will create a picture of your business.**

There have been entire books written on financing an entrepreneurial venture. That's not my mission here. My goal is to share some of my own experiences to help you create a comprehensive strategy that connects all of the pieces together, from your goals to your customers to your financials. It's important to make that connection and to recognize how, for example, resolving an operational issue will impact your financial results. I want to help you avoid a situation in which you jump into a solution without pausing to identify how it will impact your financials and the opportunities for growing your company might have.

This begins on day one. In fact, it begins before day one of the operations, as you put together the funds you'll need to start your business.

Resources for Saudi Entrepreneurs

This is an exciting time to be an entrepreneur in Saudi Arabia. The Kingdom's Vision 2030 has become the springboard for a committed and energetic approach to stimulating economic growth and ensuring that the brightest minds in the Kingdom have the resources they need to launch businesses and diversify the economy.

There are many resources available to help entrepreneurs, and as you build your business, you should investigate these to identify resources that may be most helpful.

- Small and Medium General Enterprises Authority, or Monsha'at (www.monshaat.gov.sa/en). On their site, you'll find resources to help you identify sources of funding, prepare for regulations and licensing requirements, and even answer basic questions about launching a new venture.

- Saudi Ministry of Commerce (mci.gov.sa/en) is an important resource for any entrepreneur, with links not only to licensing and regulations information but also to registering your company or brand name.

- For aspiring female entrepreneurs, the international SheTrades network (www.SheTrades.com) offers a platform for women-owned businesses to sell products and services, source from women-owned businesses, and participate in workshops and trade fairs.

Every aspect of your business, from its funding to the employees you hire (if any) and the location you choose, goes back to that very first question I encouraged you to ask at the beginning of this book: ***What is the problem you are going to solve?***

Whether you use your own funds you've saved and receive funds from family and friends as your first investors, or raise startup funds from angel investors or venture capitalists, stems back to you identifying precisely what you want from your business. Do you want to be the world's most successful high-end restaurant or a popular food truck that earns enough money that you can be comfortable and pay your bills with a bit left over?

I think most entrepreneurs when they launch a startup, want it to be big. There are, of course, a few entrepreneurs whose vision is more modest—some might say more realistic—but most of us want to be another Google or Amazon. We are thinking about world domination, not funding a nice holiday once a year. I don't think there is a right way forward. I think each enterprise, each entity, has to fulfill the financial need of the person whose vision started the project without losing sight of their passion as well.

A friend of mine told me an anecdote a few days ago that is connected to this. A multibillionaire retires and decides to go to an island to relax and enjoy his success. He buys a wonderful luxury home on the island. One day, walking along the beach, he sees a fisherman getting ready to go out on his fishing boat. It's a beautiful day, the fisherman seems to be happy to be heading out on the boat, so the billionaire asks if he could join him. The fisherman agrees and invites him to come along for the fishing expedition.

They sail out onto the water as the sun is rising. The waves are gentle, and after they get out a certain distance from the land, they start to fish. They quickly catch several large fish, at which point the fisherman prepares to return to shore.

"Are you going back already?" the billionaire asks.

"Yes," the fisherman replies. "I've caught what I need to eat."

"Why don't you catch more?" the billionaire asks. "You could sell the extra fish."

"Why would I do that?" the fisherman asks.

"You'll make more money. Maybe enough to buy a bigger fishing boat."

"Why would I want a bigger boat?"

"Well," the billionaire explains, "you can grow your business. You can buy a fleet of boats. You can catch more fish. You could even start exporting your fish all over the world."

Again, the fisherman asks, "Why would I want to do that?" "You'll have enough to buy whatever you want," the billionaire

explains. "You can become wealthy and buy a big house on the beach when you retire—just like me."

"I see," says the fisherman. "And then I can ask another fisherman to go out on the boat with him to fish."

That story made me laugh when I heard it, and it's a helpful reminder that your vision for your business matters. If your goal is to build that fishing empire, great. If it's to make enough to have a satisfying meal, also great. Your financial decision-making will be shaped by that vision, and so it will form an important pillar of your strategic framework.

One thing I've learned is that you can't be everything to everyone. Even in this book, there's so much to the entrepreneurship journey, and I could write entire volumes on funding a business, creating a brand, and growing and scaling a successful venture. But it all comes down to that strategic framework you put in place at the beginning—those core questions about the value you are going to create. These decisions will make or break your ability to succeed as an entrepreneur, and financing is one of the most vital pillars of that framework.

Know What You Need to Know

One of the things I realized early on is that I want to be an expert in my business's financial health. I want to understand the numbers, interpret them, and be able to explain them to others.

There are plenty of courses at universities designed to support financial knowledge—finance for the nonfinance person—if this is something that you also find challenging. I've chosen to enroll in the Chartered Financial Analyst (CFA) Institute certification program. It's an international organization that provides rigorous educational programs in investments and finance, with training and resources designed to inform you of the leading thought leadership on all aspects of finance. In order to earn the CFA certification, you must pass three very challenging exams, each of which requires about three hundred hours of study.

I would love to earn that certification—it's an internationally recognized symbol of the very best financial minds in the world. But I don't need to earn it. There are only about 120 of those CFA certificate holders in the entire Kingdom! I don't intend to become a financial analyst, but I know that if I invest the time in the curriculum and resources, and learn enough to pass the exam, I'll be very satisfied. My goal is to be able to form a complete picture of my business's financials so that I can then identify someone who is strong enough to handle those finances for me while I focus on what I love, which is operations and growth.

One thing the CFA course has inspired me to do is to think more strategically about the three financial statements that make up your venture's financials: the cash flow, the balance sheet, and the profit and loss. Most people spend a lot of time talking about the profit and loss statements, but I love how they're all integrated together, and how a number in the profit and loss statement is reflected in the balance sheet. Those numbers are cross-referenced among the financial statements; there's clear integration. When I study the sales figures or the operational costs, there's a connection. Cash flow creates the numbers that find their way onto the balance sheet. It's very synergistic.

An example of this occurred when we had to sell one of our car repair workshops because we were moving to a new location with a bigger capacity. And that led us to the logical question: How much should we sell the workshop for?

This wasn't something that requires an instinct. I needed to know what a logical asking price would be, as well as the number below which I would walk away from the transaction. I needed to understand how that asset—the workshop—sits on my balance sheet. When I looked at the numbers, I could recognize my walkaway price, the price below which I would be losing money. That's the point where it impacts the profit and loss statement. Understanding that number really pushed me in my negotiations, because I knew that there was a sweet spot, a price that, if I received it, would have a nice impact on my cash flow.

Sir Francis Bacon famously said that "knowledge itself is power," and I can tell you that I felt quite powerful when I went back to my team armed with a clear understanding of how the negotiated price for our workshop would impact the entire business's financials. I knew that the workshop sale meant we would reduce the holding costs of our assets on our balance sheet. I knew that the sales price meant an injection of cash that needed to be included in our cash flow. I recognized that the difference between the holding cost of the asset and its sales price must be reflected in our profit and loss statement.

I've seen many entrepreneurs struggle at navigating the question of cash flow. Your payments and the way that you pay your suppliers and the way you receive money from your customers do not always align neatly. Sometimes you have to put money into the business to keep operations going until your revenue catches up. My leases and rent, for example, must be paid six months in advance. I have to pay my staff and my suppliers. These are expenses before any customers have paid their bills—and customers will find a million reasons not to pay you.

It's critical to understand the nuances of your cash flow. You need to know how much you are going to spend this week, next week, next month, and in two more months. You need to be able to predict the money that will come into the business and try to match it to the money going out.

I use an extremely simple, unsophisticated system to track this and make it as clear and easy as possible. I use an Excel sheet that tracks by month and shows how much I want to spend on rent, how much I want to spend on my staff, how much on marketing, and how much on equipment. These are expenses that I can control.

As soon as you understand how much cash you will be spending, you can focus on your sales. It's not simply a matter of selling enough products or services to make $5,000 or $10,000 or $100,000 this month. What's important is knowing when you will receive that money and what actions you need to take until you do.

As entrepreneurs, we want to focus on the creative process—on identifying solutions and determining the best way to get what we have created to the customers who need it. But successful entrepreneurs recognize that they are not simply creating a product or service; they are building a business to sustain that creation.

I realize that I am just beginning to scratch the surface of understanding financials, but what I'm learning and sharing with my team is informing our ability to think much more strategically about every business decision. It impacted a recent discussion about parking. We've been looking for a solution to our need for more parking, and the team came to me after finding a location. They explained that it offered ample parking for X number of dollars per spot, and it was in a convenient location. This, they told me, would immediately solve our parking problem.

My first questions centered not around parking or customer service but finances: "How will this affect us financially? This will be an additional cost for us that the customer will not pay for. Why should we incur it?"

The team wasn't initially able to respond, but what followed was a very interesting discussion. They began to examine the problem strategically around a key question: Why do we need this additional parking in the first place? The answer, we realized, was because our customers were often late in picking up their cars.

One solution was for customers to be charged for late pickups. Those charges could offset the cost of the additional parking access, potentially even generating a small profit.

These discussions energized the team because they directly linked their performance and their solutions to the overall financial profitability of the company. It was a helpful reminder to recognize how operational problems—and solutions—are directly connected to financial statements. It also demonstrated how you can have a smoothly running operation that begins to lose money.

With any decision like this, it's also helpful to pause and reflect on your core mission for your company. If your business is shaped by quick turnaround, you'll want to institute procedures that encourage cars to move in and out of your workshop swiftly. If your value statement is centered around low-cost service, you'll want to carefully assess any changes that will force you to raise prices.

You may discover that there are several strategic solutions to an operational problem. Before you jump at the first solution to that problem, step back, assess the financials, and reflect on how any solution fits within your original strategic framework.

The Daily Dashboard

One of the best, most important tools I use in my work is my daily dashboard. If you haven't created one yet for your venture, I encourage you to spend some time learning about the impact it can have on your ability to display, analyze, and track your business's key performance indicators. A daily dashboard is basically a snapshot of how your business is performing right now.

There are plenty of dashboard templates available to download, but it's helpful to customize one that tracks the metrics that matter most to you.

It should include high-level information you can use to make critical decisions. Those key performance indicators that are impacting your business every day—that's what your dashboard must include, in the information that's easy to see quickly. Note that I said "every day." Your dashboard should include that information that needs to be checked on a daily basis. It might include any gaps between your target and actual revenue for the week, a tally of the number of new customers you've serviced that month, or a report on the average revenue per customer compared with that same number last month or last year.

The dashboard shouldn't be a static report of numbers; it should include charts or graphics to provide context and enable you to make decisions without waiting for disappointing end-of-quarter or end-of-year results. When you look at a profit and loss statement, for example, you'll see how much money you made or spent. But as an entrepreneur, you need to know the why behind those numbers so you can make adjustments and increase or change your strategy if necessary.

Financial reports are like a scoreboard. They tell you the end results, but they don't tell you how you played the game. A daily dashboard gives you that context. It tells you what you did well and where you need to improve. It's a way to track whether you're achieving the numbers that will help you hit your targets for the month. As you use them, you'll learn that, for example, if you haven't hit your numbers by the fifth day of the month, there's an issue that you need to correct. It may be a supply chain issue. You can then find out if it's a problem specific to you or a wide issue. If it's a wider issue, you might decide to source those parts more quickly from an external source. It might be more expensive, but if you're the only business that has access to those parts, you'll be able to charge a bit more for them.

Financial reports are like a scoreboard. They tell you the end results, but they don't tell you how you played the game.

That's what I like about the daily dashboard. It basically tells you how well you're playing the game—before it's too late, before the end of the month. It gives you time to determine what's happening and what needs to be fixed. It gives you the knowledge you'll need to take action.

I work with three dashboards. I build my first dashboard around my revenue. Costs are fixed. You can control your costs, but revenues you don't control them because they come from external sources. I want to carefully track my performance based on the knowledge that I need to achieve X amount to generate the profits that I'm looking for. These are the metrics I track in my operational dashboard.

The second dashboard is a supplier dashboard. With that, I'm tracking my supply chain, how much I will need to pay suppliers, and how much I've already paid them.

The third dashboard is my collection dashboard. This one tracks the money I'm receiving from my customers. It's broken down into thirty days, sixty days, and ninety days. That gives me the understanding to say to my team, for example, "Next month is going to be a tough month for us. We don't have enough cash to pay our suppliers, so go manage them." And by managing them, I mean, picking up a phone and having a conversation. Telling them that we won't be able to pay their full bill at the end of the month, but we can pay 25 percent. They will be upset, but not as much as they would be at the end of the month. You're giving them time to prepare and adjust. When you tell them bad news up front, it's more manageable. They'll also respect you for your honesty and for giving them that time. It's always a matter of making adjustments on our end so that, going forward, we can pay them fully. The daily dashboards aren't simply a resource for me. They're a communication tool. I share them with the whole team. I want them to understand our performance to recognize how they are contributing to those results. I want them to see the importance of taking action to achieve targets.

I have my dashboards live, and I'm constantly tracking them. That's why I like Google spreadsheets—they're updated instantly. Money collected from customers is reflected the moment it goes into the bank account. Every day at 5:00 p.m., when we shut down, the performance for that day is updated—the number of cars we serviced, the job orders that closed, and the number of cars we received. We have a dashboard that reflects the spare parts we need to source for the next day or the next week to repair the cars that we have in our workshops.

I use it for the daily huddles I hold with my team. They know that my questions will be based on the data I'm monitoring in real-time. I can see much more than money going out and coming in. I can see the why and the how, and I know what needs to change in order to achieve the results I'm expecting.

Always an Opportunity to Get it Right

One of the things I learned from Rebecca Homkes was the idea of a strategy cycle. A strategy cycle is essentially a framework that an organization can use to regularly coordinate operations and budget. It's a way to check and make sure that you're getting it right, that you're playing the game well and achieving your goals.

Depending on the maturity of your company, this strategy cycle should be about three years. Every three years, you should stop and reassess. Are you continuing to effectively solve the problems that you want to solve? Have your customers' needs changed? Do you need to change your original assumptions?

Your daily dashboard should enable you to track this performance and recognize its context within this overall strategic framework. You want to be able to continue to test your assumptions and determine whether or not the actions you're taking are working as you intended them to. If not, you can then revisit that assumption and determine why not.

We always tend to focus more on the negative than the positive, but the daily dashboard is also a great tool to help you recognize and celebrate wins. Did you exceed the number of new customers you needed to welcome to your business this month? That should be something you celebrate. Is a new product more successful than you expected? Again, that's something to celebrate.

Your financing and your daily dashboard are the scoreboards you can use to track your successes and to confirm that you are operating as you want within the strategic framework you've created. But the financials are equally important before you launch your business.

It's challenging to pivot from idea to data, but it's a critical pivot to make. Once you clarify your fixed expenses, you can make decisions that will shape your business. Your strategic framework has helped you identify your ideal customer and the service you'll provide them; the financials then tell you how many of those ideal customers you'll need and how much revenue you'll need to earn from them in order to meet your expenses and become profitable. They will help you clarify what profit you're expecting and what actions you'll need to take in order to receive it.

An understanding of your financials will equip you to think strategically about what you'll need to start your business. It will inform your decisions about location, equipment, and—as we'll discuss in the next chapter—who you need to hire to achieve your goals.

Chapter Six

Who are the People You Need on Your Team?

"Proactively seeking and employing the most talented people can have a multiplier effect on the creation of other competitive advantages."

—BRADFORD D. SMAR

ONE OF THE MOST IMPORTANT strategic decisions you will make as you launch your company comes as you begin to identify the right people for your goals. I've learned not only to think carefully about who to hire but also when. Let me explain.

Many entrepreneurs start hiring before they've built out the strategic framework we've discussed in previous chapters. They want to put their team in place before they've carefully researched industry dynamics, with the intent that the people they hire can then help them identify key aspects of their strategy.

My suggestion is to reverse this process—to let your strategy determine who will be right for you to hire, rather than allowing the people you've hired to determine the right strategy. Without fully understanding how you're going to compete and forming a clear financial picture, it's impossible to make strategic hiring decisions. If you're going to compete on speed and quality of service, you need skilled technicians. If you're entering a competitive marketplace, you need a talented marketing specialist and a knowledgeable sales team. If you're competing with lower pricing, you may not be able to afford expensive hires.

The same strategy that has informed your decision-making throughout this process should be used as you determine who you need to contribute to your success. I think of it as if I'm the manager of a competitive sports team. If I'm entering an arena where the competition is consistently scoring goal after goal, I'm going to make sure that I hire a skilled goalkeeper. Defenders and strikers matter, of course, but my team must include at least one goalkeeper in order to compete successfully.

Many entrepreneurs are tempted to hire friends when they launch a business. I understand completely. It's comfortable to work with people whom we know, who understand us, and with whom we have a lot in common. But I've learned that I never want to have to fire a friend if they're not performing or if they don't have the skills I need for a specific task or challenge. I'd rather keep that wall of separation between friend and employee!

When it comes to hiring, I do turn to my network to find the right people, but in a slightly different way. I ask for referrals. I'm specific and clear about the skills I need and the salary I can pay, and I know that I can trust my friends to put me in touch with candidates who fit my criteria. I have several friends who are smart and trustworthy chief financial officers. When I'm launching a business that needs a CFO,

I don't hire my friends, but I do ask them to recommend someone—perhaps someone they've worked with, someone they respect.

As an entrepreneur, you're managing so many different responsibilities that it's tempting to hire quickly once you've identified specific roles that you need to fill. It's also tempting to fire slowly. Firing an underperforming employee is never easy—and, as we just discussed, it can be much harder in a small organization made up of friends and family.

In fact, this seems to be the rule of thumb for many businesses I know: hire fast and fire slow. I believe in hiring slowly and carefully. As for firing, I'm going to say something that may be controversial, especially at a time when businesses are struggling to fill jobs: I don't think we fire fast enough.

I've seen many leaders take their time to find the right people, invest the time to train them, and then place them in key roles. Then, when they discover after a few months that those individuals are struggling, many companies decide that they need to place them in a different role. They've invested the time and money to recruit, hire, and train these people, so instead of letting them go, they shift them to a different department. The idea is that if they didn't work in payroll, let's move them into procurement. Maybe they will find themselves there.

In my experience, this never works. You're not thinking strategically. You're simply taking an individual and then trying to find a role they can play. If you've taken your time to define a position and find a person who has the specific skills you need, they should be able to perform successfully within a few months. If not, you should always be prepared to fire them.

Does this seem inhumane to you? Are you hesitating at the idea of firing people quickly? I actually think it's much more ethical to fire people in this way. I'd much prefer to be very specific about what I need from a role and let someone know that they aren't able to meet a very clear and targeted set of requirements rather than shuffle them from one role to another, none of which are a perfect fit.

When we're launching a startup, we need people who can work collaboratively and fill multiple roles. We need people who want to get involved in different aspects of the business. If I discover that I've hired someone who is talented but needs more structure and who can excel only when doing a clear set of tasks every day, that's not a good fit for my startup. That's someone who will excel in a larger or more established company. They're going to suffer working for my startup because they won't be comfortable in that culture. But if they move to a competitor of ours, a very structured, very hierarchical organization, they might be able to thrive.

I've encountered this situation more than once, most recently with a financial manager. They struggled in our organization despite having all the skills for the job on paper. In this case, we needed someone to manage certain specific responsibilities, very task-oriented, and this individual was eager to test out new approaches and install new processes. For that company and that role, it wasn't a good fit, so I had to let him go. Today, he's an entrepreneur successfully running his own business selling safety equipment. We're still in touch, and I can tell you that he's much happier.

Of course, your firing decisions must be shaped by the local employment laws in place in the country in which you launch your business. Here in Saudi Arabia, the law allows a probation period of three months that can be extended to an additional six months.

Beyond the legal requirements, there are also your own expectations for how quickly you want your employees to get up to speed and begin performing. My expectation is that, if I've been thoughtful and careful in the hiring process and have thoroughly explained my requirements, the people I hire will begin delivering on day one. They won't wait to achieve. I've had some challenges with this, as you can imagine. There are always people you hire who will say things like, "I need time to learn." When they say that, it means that I'll be paying them to learn, and I'm not going to be seeing the desired outcomes I want. It may also mean that my processes are too complex and need to be simplified. As humans, we tend to overcomplicate processes, and for a business, this can be quite dangerous. If you've hired good people—people with the skills and experience to perform the job—and they are struggling to understand your systems, you may need to consider whether there's an opportunity to simplify processes to allow your team to start contributing more quickly.

As humans, we tend to overcomplicate processes, and for a business, this can be quite dangerous.

Reed Hastings, the co-founder, and co-CEO of Netflix discusses the importance of talent density. This means that your goal should be a workforce of high performers. He describes what he calls the "Keeper Test"—he identifies those individuals whom he would fight hard to keep if they told him they were leaving for a competitor. Netflix's success, according to Hastings, has come from the fact that they have a large number of very strong performers who are creating new opportunities for success for the streaming service. When you employ great people, Hastings argues, great people want to come work for you. Great people need fewer rules and less management.[1]

---

1. Reed Hastings and Erin Meyer, No Rules Rules: Netflix and the Culture of Reinvention (New York: Penguin, 2020).

I think there's an interesting lesson here for you as an entrepreneur. If you aspire to be the next Netflix, you can start by thinking of your startup less like a family and more like a team. You always want the best players—the individuals who can support the strategic framework you've created from the beginning.

Hire A-Players

Recently, I was in Paris with my wife. We both love art, and so we spent a lot of time going into different art galleries, admiring all of the art pieces.

We explored a wide range of galleries in various parts of the city, but two of them stood out. In those two galleries, a friendly salesperson approached us, made us feel welcome, and offered to help. They showed us many different pieces without pressuring us to buy or without expecting anything in return for their time and effort. The other galleries we visited had lovely pieces, but what I remember is the excellent service I received specifically in those two galleries.

At the time, we were not ready to purchase any art—but one day, we will. And we agreed that when we're ready, we will call those two salespeople.

Bradford D. Smart, in his book *Topgrading*, talks about the value of filling your organization with employees like those two salespeople. He calls them A-players.

I loved Smart's writing and found several of his principles to be helpful in thinking about how to ensure that my companies are employing top performers in all roles. One of the core concepts of the book is the importance of having clear targets and communicating them with your employees. They need to know the goal in order to demonstrate exceptional performance.

I always want to learn from other CEOs who are successful, and what both Smart and Hastings talk about is strategically assessing not just your organization and its processes but also the people you hire and promote. Whether you call them top performers or A-players, these are the people who should be forming the majority of your employees. You don't need all A-players—Smith emphasizes this in his book—but you certainly want to strive to hire the best, promote the best, and train and coach all employees to do their best.

It's an interesting exercise, one that you can practice wherever you are, whether it's an art gallery, an auto repair business, or a coffee shop. Pay attention to the people who are interacting with customers, to those who are providing services, to those who are stocking shelves and keeping waiting areas clean. You'll find it's easier than you may have thought to spot the A-players—and the B-, C-, and D-players too.

I talked earlier about wanting to earn a five-star Google review. I want to exceed my customer's expectations. And I want my employees to recognize the value of ensuring that their attitudes and actions are not simply customer oriented for the individuals they are serving today but oriented toward future customers as well.

By now, you probably know that I'm a car enthusiast. Recently, I was at a dinner and saw someone who had a Lamborghini parked outside. It was a beautiful car, and so of course I went up and was chatting with the owner about his car. I learned that he was a Lamborghini distributor. Our conversation was interrupted by a security guard, who told us that there was a man who was asking for permission to take a picture of the car.

My companion immediately agreed. In fact, he gestured to the man to come over, opened the car door for him, invited him to sit inside the car, and suggested that he also take a video to post on social media. The man was thrilled—he had simply hoped to take a picture of the exterior of the car, and instead, he left that encounter with a video of himself seated in the driver's seat of that wonderful car.

"Thank you for doing that," I told the man. "He will never forget that experience."

"Of course," he replied. "He may be my customer someday."

It's such an interesting lesson in thinking strategically and investing in people and relationships. I don't know whether or not that Lamborghini distributor will ever encounter the man who wanted the photo. But the point is neither did he. You don't know who your customers will be in a year, or five years. Neither do your employees. If and when that man becomes successful, he will remember the experience, remember the friendliness, remember what it felt like to spend time in that beautiful car and to be treated with courtesy by its owner. A-players know the value of being humble and kind and of treating others with respect. They are willing to invest in others and exceed expectations in every relationship.

Hire Good People... Who Make Others Better

Another aspect of hiring strategically comes as you recognize that the best employees elevate the rest of the organization. Loyal, friendly, hardworking employees inspire others to perform at their best. Your strategic hiring should be focused on the goal of filling your company with these kinds of team members.

Robert Sutton has a memorable way of describing this strategy. When I tell you the title of his book, it will become clear. Sutton's book is *The No Asshole Rule*, and his writing focuses on building a plan to create what he calls a "civilized workplace." Sutton's philosophy is that organizations that eliminate these toxic employees, either by firing them or simply not hiring them in the first place, are not simply more civilized—they are more productive and successful as well.

You can replace Sutton's term with whatever phrase is most comfortable for you. The point is to avoid those individuals whose actions and behavior are negatively impacting your company.

Sutton's rule was first expressed in an article published in *Harvard Business Review*. That's where I encountered it, and honestly, it really resonated with me, not because of a candidate that I was thinking about hiring, but because of someone I had already hired.

This guy was a high performer, very successful, and was contributing a significant amount of revenue to the company. But he was a nightmare to work with. People were constantly complaining about him. It was a struggle because I knew that if I got rid of him, we would lose a lot of money, but the entire organization would be much happier.

Sutton's article helped me to recognize that even though as a leader I was ultimately responsible for hiring and firing decisions, this was a decision that would impact the organization as a whole. As such, I should engage my team in deciding the right course of action and determining how to navigate the aftermath.

So I talked to my team. They were familiar with the complaints, but I clarified the financial impact. They quickly came up with a solution: we would get rid of the one person who was negatively impacting the workplace, and they would work collectively to make up the difference and pick up the slack.

It was fantastic. We fired the high performer who was making everyone miserable. The employees were happy, the customers were happy, and we were able to ensure that the revenue did not dip when he departed.

It's a good lesson, one that I encourage you to remember. You don't need to employ assholes, no matter how successful they may be at certain aspects of their job.

Elon Musk, the CEO of SpaceX and Tesla, uses this principle as a way to ensure that the people he employs will fit well into his organization. When asked how he identifies who to hire, Musk said, "Generally, I look for a positive attitude, and are they easy to work with, are people going to like working with them? It's very important to like the people you work with, otherwise life [and] your job are gonna be quite miserable. And, in fact, we have a strict no-assholes policy at SpaceX. And we fire people if they are."[2]

Elon Musk's comments reflect the fact that the people you choose to hire will depend on the culture you want to create. Someone who may be an asshole in one organization can thrive in another with a different set of values.

---

2. Marcel Schwantes, "Elon Musk's 'No a--Hole' Policy at SpaceX Is a Great Example of Whom You Should Hire and Fire," Inc.com (Inc., July 9, 2021), https://www.inc.com/marcel-schwantes/elon-musks-no-a-hole-poli cy-at-spacex-is-a-great-example-of-who-you-should-hire-fire.html

I'm forty-three years old now, and one of the things I've asked myself lately is what can I do to eliminate any negative energy around me. I'm noticing that my ankles and knees need a little more time to warm up when I'm doing something physical. I'm becoming smarter about taking steps to pay attention to those goals that inspire energy and the people who add to that energy.

The same thing should be true for your organization. As you build your teams, it's critical to acknowledge the importance of how people make you and others feel. That's why I've become a strong believer in implementing the no-asshole rule.

Who Do You Hire?

I promised to share my real experiences, to help you learn from me what has worked and what didn't. The advice I'm sharing here is advice I often had to learn the hard way, through research, asking questions of experts and fellow entrepreneurs, and trying to do better the next time.

So here goes. I've shared the importance of strategic hiring in this chapter, but in one of my first ventures, the strategy I used for hiring people was simple. Essentially, if they had a pulse and showed up for an interview, they were hired.

I've learned a lot since then, and one of the most important lessons was this: identify what your organization needs to succeed strategically and hire based on that framework. Early on, I learned that the person I most needed to hire in order to succeed was a person to make key hiring decisions! In fact, I needed a smart and experienced HR manager. I discovered that I wasn't as effective as I needed to be during hiring interviews. I always tended to see the good in people, identifying their strengths and overlooking their weaknesses. I realized that it was important to have more than one person interview job candidates to form a more complete picture of who we'd be hiring. I've discovered that it can be helpful to have their potential peers participate in the interview process; I'm even considering having their subordinates participate, possibly by chatting with them over a cup of coffee. As an entrepreneur with many competing priorities, you'll need to quickly identify your business's existing strengths and hire for your weaknesses. If you're great at finding good people, and talented contributors who can support your strategic framework, congratulations. If not, that's a key position that you need to fill.

Many HR managers hire based on a job description—simplifying a role into a few key skills and then hiring based on that checklist. We've all been guilty of writing a job description that is more about background and experience than skills. But what you need to know is, twelve months from now, what will this individual deliver to your organization? If I'm hiring a financial manager, I expect to have my financials ready by the first day of each month. I expect to be informed if I need to secure funding or manage cash flow.

What does that mean? Let's say that I have three months of cash in my bank account. That's my ready cash in case anything goes wrong—money I can use to pay salaries. I want my financial manager to oversee that every day, to keep me fully informed so that I can anticipate, instead of react to, any problems that may arise.

It's hard to put that into a job description. Job descriptions can give you an idea of the role you may be stepping into, but what I want to know is what you will actually do in that role. My HR managers know this and know to ask questions to find out how every candidate is going to contribute to making our companies better. Their approach is straightforward. They communicate the key performance indicators (KPIs) for the job based on our strategic framework. They tell candidates what they are, explaining that this is what's needed, and then ask, "Are you able to achieve this?"

As you identify the roles you need to fill in your organization, don't just describe the job. Identify the KPIs. And then, when you're interviewing candidates, ask them if they can deliver these KPIs.

I've learned that good hiring—strategic hiring—should be centered around measurable goals: KPIs, numbers, and markers that will enable you and your employees to see how close or how far they are from achieving the organization's goals. Those shouldn't be mysteries or something you save for the onboarding process. I want every person I hire to be fully prepared for what they're going to face on the job and confident in their ability to manage it. If our cash flow is in a crunch and we're going to have a few challenging months, I want any prospective hire to be aware of this and ready to do what's needed. If we're a startup with a need for people to fill many different roles and dedicate extra hours to launching a venture, I want to make sure that the people I hire can thrive in that environment.

I want every person I hire to be fully prepared for what they're going to face on the job and confident in their ability to manage it.

Hiring Questions Every Entrepreneur Should Use

When I'm hiring team members, I remember that I'm going to be spending at least eight hours a day with that person. That's often more time than I spend with my family.

There are key hiring questions my HR managers use to make sure that employees have the skills we need to contribute on day one. But there are also a few factors I assess—factors that you may find helpful to consider as you begin hiring.

1. What are the KPIs for this role?

2. Will this individual be able to work toward those KPIs on day one?

3. One year from now, how will I measure the success of this hire?

4. Is this person as driven as I am?

5. Is this just a job for them, or an opportunity to achieve a specific life goal?

Recruit or Promote

In this chapter, we've focused a lot on the idea of external hiring decisions. But it's also important to elevate internal employees—to identify existing people who have the skills and ability to step up into a higher-level position.

In my conversations with other CEOs, I've heard some argue strongly for the value of bringing "new blood" into an organization as a way to bring innovation, new knowledge, and new ways of thinking. My preference is always to look internally first, to identify ways to develop my own teams to reward their loyalty and encourage them to continue to grow. But it has to be done carefully. I also know too many organizations that promoted a successful salesman to a sales director just because that was the common way to reward successful sales levels without stopping to assess whether this person had the necessary skills to manage others.

I would love every person I hire to eventually be so successful that they are promoted. But my organizational structure doesn't work that way. Not many do. In fact, most organizations are structured in a pyramid. There's one person at the top, one CEO spot. Not everyone gets to become the CEO; not every successful employee has the skills to manage other people.

An idea I've been developing is with our vehicle service centers. This idea is still in the early stages, but I'll share the process that's being iterated as I write this book. We need to hire a lot of mechanics— many of them are smart and talented, but their career path is limited. What I'm working toward is a hybrid of a franchise model with a career path. We'll hire entry-level mechanics and, after two years, provide an opportunity for them to build the skills to operate their own franchise.

I think that this could be a very interesting model, especially as a way to respond to the challenge of making sure that the pipeline is continually filled with talented, ambitious, hardworking mechanics. I am looking into the possibility of working with technical institutes to recruit for the project. I need to make sure that it fits into the organization's strategic framework and that I have the financials to support it. Yes, this is still a work in progress, but I think it could be an exciting way to hire the best.

Can You Automate?

One lesson I've learned as my businesses grow is that throwing more people at a problem isn't necessarily the right way forward. Too often, as we scale, as we explore new markets, or assess potential new sources of revenue, my teams quickly recommend hiring someone—or several people. The thinking is that more people will enable you to expand and take advantage of new opportunities.

Before you move too quickly to expand your staff, take time to pause and consider whether you might be able to automate some part of your processes instead. Let's suppose that you've determined that your existing accounts payable team is stretched too thin. You decide to hire an additional accounts-payable staff member. Then a member of the accounts payable team goes on leave, and you need to hire another person to manage their workload. Instead of moving in this direction, with multiple people and an increasingly complex process, it may be worth investigating whether parts of your existing accounts payable process could be automated.

This situation has cropped up more than once for me—in fact, just before writing this chapter, it happened again. My finance manager came to me and said that we needed to hire more people to do the work. When I questioned him, he listed many different tasks that had to be performed, and with the holidays approaching, we were balancing a challenging workload with minimal staff in place to handle the work. He explained that our existing systems needed many interventions and a lot of manipulation in order to ensure that payments were processed correctly.

This suggested that the problem was a lack of correct automation, not a lack of enough people. Accounting is straightforward. You have suppliers you need to pay. You have customers you need to invoice. It's not that complicated.

This led to a lively discussion about whether we were focusing on the most cost-efficient way to accomplish these important functions. If our systems weren't functioning properly, that was where we needed to start. Now we are in the process of upgrading all of our financial software systems. The new products we're installing are more efficient—and logical. It will no longer take three months to train staff in how to use them; the onboarding and training are much easier. It's no longer a crisis when a member of the team needs to take leave, and the financial team is able to generate invoices and track payments more efficiently.

Finding The Right Partners

Because the focus of this chapter is on finding the right people for your goals, I wanted to take a few minutes to share some thoughts on how to find the right partners for your venture. Obviously, as an entrepreneur, you may need partners to help you launch your business, either as cofounders or as investors. How do you do this, and what makes a successful partnership?

A smart CEO once told me, when we were discussing potential partnerships, that he viewed it like a deeply committed marriage. You enter into it with high hopes, and you do all that's necessary to avoid ever getting divorced.

This idea stuck with me. I do think partnerships require a significant long-term commitment. You never want a partner whose decision-making is impacted by a plan to get as much profit out of the business as quickly as possible.

But I also think you need to be strategic in your partnerships. You need to consider what this individual brings to the table—what skills or knowledge or connections do they have that will supplement and enhance those that you already have?

If you're considering a potential partnership, stop and first consider those two questions and be very clear from the beginning on the answers: Will this be a long-term partnership? What do I expect to get out of this relationship?

I've had to ask myself these questions more than once. Many foreign companies are interested in a potential Saudi partner. Let's take technology as one example. In Saudi Arabia, we're going through significant digitization, with smart cities investing in AI. And investing in a technology partnership sounds fun if I'm honest. But I've learned to go back to the strategic framework, to ask those critical questions and examine the financials. There are significant costs and development fees to technology projects, and many of these foreign partnerships create structures so that any profits generated end up with the foreign investor, while the Saudi costs are such that a project of that scale would be barely breaking even.

There's a perception among many foreign companies that the Saudi market is rich with potential—it's a great place to make a lot of money. While they're looking at the dollar signs, we're instead looking for ideas that will build something for the future. If you're an entrepreneur, you understand this mindset.

Please recognize that I'm sharing my perspective to equip you to ask the right questions. Not all foreign partnerships are wrong. If you can identify someone who will add value to your venture, who is aligned with your goals, and who believes in what you are trying to accomplish, that's a fantastic relationship.

Don't be afraid to ask strategic questions to confirm that any potential partners share your mission and values for your company. My father taught me when I was starting out, to enter any partnership knowing the best way in—and the best way out. If your intent is for this to be a long-term relationship, your contracts should be negotiated with those exit clauses designed to support this goal. The partnership will be stronger and more effective if you begin it understanding how and when you will exit. You'll want any agreement to clarify any expectations you may have, reflecting what might happen if your market changes, if your outcomes are not what you expected, or if someone wants to acquire your company. Have an open and frank discussion about these potential exits from the beginning as a way to confirm that you are in agreement about how the partnership will evolve. Consider areas of potential conflict, knowing that you're hoping that they don't arise but will be prepared if they do.

Be equally clear about whether this investor is the right person for your unique goals. Are they providing an infusion of much-needed cash? What else? Are they bringing knowledge of a core business? Potential customers?

Many entrepreneurs I talk with mention that it's easy to be strategic when you're talking about numbers but much harder when you're talking about people. I understand. I've wrestled with identifying the best partners for a venture. I've made mistakes and learned from them when it comes to hiring the right people—and the wrong people. What I've learned is that every aspect of your business should be examined through that strategic framework, including the people. Be clear about your goals for your business, understand how and where you will compete, and use that knowledge to identify the people who will position you for success.

Part IV

Overcome the Pitfalls Along the Startup Journey

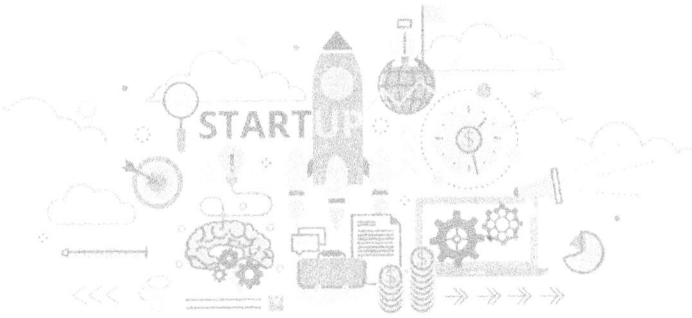

Chapter Seven

What Are The Potential Pitfalls to Success?

"I'm convinced that about half of what separates successful entrepreneurs from the non-successful ones is pure perseverance."

—STEVE JOBS

I SOMETIMES THINK that the biggest challenge many entrepreneurs face is not the process of launching their business but what comes next. Most entrepreneurs spend months, even years, preparing for that first day of operations. They've studied their market, identified their competitive advantage, and researched their financials. They've found a location, purchased equipment, and possibly hired employees. It's a heady experience to open for business and to welcome your first customers.

I've shared in this book a strategic framework that can equip you to prepare for this process more thoughtfully. But you must be every bit as strategic moving forward, implementing your plans and integrating systems to continue to check and track your progress.

There are many different ways in which you can monitor your success that I've found helpful. I'll share them in this chapter. As a leader, you must track your progress as well as that of your company. It's tempting to focus only on the data—which, of course, is critical! But you also need to ensure that your leadership style is enabling the success of your organization. If it isn't, you want to take action to correct what isn't working. As an entrepreneur, you propelled your company into existence with your vision, but as your organization grows, you need to transition and grow from an entrepreneur into a leader, and this can be challenging.

I mentioned earlier that I rely on trusted advisors to give me feedback, share their insights and recommendations, and offer advice when I encounter a challenge. But the best people who give you feedback on the effectiveness of your leadership style are your employees, the individuals who you want to lead.

The best people who give you feedback on the effectiveness of your leadership style are your employees, the individuals who you want to lead.

In order to ensure that the feedback I'm getting as a leader is honest and unbiased, I use the 360-degree feedback method developed by executive coach Marshall Goldsmith. Goldsmith is the author of many insightful business books. He's coached CEOs and C-suite executives from some of the top companies in the world (such as Ford Motor Company and GlaxoSmithKline) in how to become stronger and more successful leaders, and his 360-degree feedback strategy has helped me learn when and where to pivot to become a better CEO.

At its heart, Goldsmith's 360-degree feedback method is designed to provide a way for you to gather and implement feedback from others in your organization. Some companies use it for executives at the C-suite level, while other organizations implement it more widely as a tool to gather insights from peers and superiors.

Goldsmith's methodology is designed to enable you to assess your performance in people-related and results-related areas. It focuses on fifteen key leadership areas that Goldsmith has identified as being critical for success as a leader:

- Demonstrating integrity

- Encouraging constructive dialogue

- Creating a shared vision

- Developing people

- Building partnerships

- Sharing leadership

- Empowering people

- Thinking globally

- Appreciating diversity

- Developing technological savvy

- Ensuring customer satisfaction

- Maintaining a competitive advantage

- Achieving personal mastery

- Anticipating opportunities[1]

Before we go any further in this discussion, I encourage you to take a minute and really study that list. Think about your own leadership. Do any areas jump out at you, either as personal strengths or weaknesses? As an entrepreneur, you likely are devoting focus to ensuring customer satisfaction and maintaining a competitive advantage; but as you transition into a leader of a thriving business, you can see from this list that there are many areas for potential personal growth, areas that will become critical as your company scales up and the team you are managing expands.

Check Your Leadership Skills

Many companies conduct annual performance reviews for employees. I've learned that it's helpful for me, as a leader, to get this kind of feedback on my performance. I use a version of the 360-degree feedback method developed by executive coach Marshall Goldsmith and request feedback from my team in five key areas:

- My ability to communicate effectively

- My success in engaging people

- My commitment to empowering other leaders

- My actions to ensure the company's success

---

1. "Global Leadership Assessment (GLA 360) the Best 360 Degree Assessment," New Age Leader- ship, July 9, 2021, https://newagelead ership.com/gla360/.

- My skills in anticipating and responding to change

These are the competencies that will ensure that you are continuing to grow and evolve as a leader. There are many variations of these 360-degree feedback assessments. I encourage you to find one that works well for your business and invite meaningful feedback from those with whom you work.

What's interesting about 360-degree feedback, unlike some typical performance reviews, is that it's gathered from multiple sources—including yourself! Some leaders request feedback from peers, employees, and even customers. The idea behind gathering and examining reports from many different individuals is that multiple reports from different viewpoints are more likely to give you a clearer picture of your strengths and weaknesses than feedback from just one person. When you compare how you assess yourself with how others perceive you, you can build very helpful knowledge. What's critical is to not simply read the feedback but to use that feedback to set some specific goals for yourself. As you identify opportunities for growth, you can create a three-month, six-month, and one-year set of challenges for yourself to ensure that you are becoming more effective.

I completed my latest 360-degree review a few months ago. I love this process so much that I'm going to implement it with my C-suite-level team next year. The feedback I receive is anonymous; it comes from peers and direct reports. I also assess myself and then compare all the results.

I promised to share my true experiences with you, and because I'm committed to that transparency, I'll share the key takeaways from my results. My two biggest challenges this year—the areas on which I'll be working to improve my results—are that I'm handling too many projects at once, and I need to work on delegating tasks in order to focus more on the operational aspects of the business. I appreciate this feedback; it shows that my team recognizes that I'm trying to contribute positively to them and to our venture, but I've overcommitted and need to streamline my workload.

It can be challenging in a smaller organization to ensure that there is a sense of anonymity so that people will be able to be honest in assessing you. But my focus, with this kind of assessment, is not to provide a vehicle for people to complain or compliment. No, what I want to know is, What is Husam good at, and what does he need to stop doing? I use an HR consultant to direct the process and to help me accurately interpret the feedback I get.

As a leader, I want to know how I'm seen and how effective I am. You'll want to remember, as your business grows, that your strategic leadership is as important to your business's health as your profits and losses.

A great place to get started is with six central questions that Marshall Goldsmith often uses with his clients. These questions have inspired some lively discussions with my team, and as you'll see, they are clearly linked to the strategic framework you've been building for your business:

1. Where are we going?

2. Where are you going?

3. What is going well?

4. Where can we improve?

5. How can I help you?

6. How can you help me?[2]

Take Your Punches and Keep Going

As an entrepreneur, I've learned that no matter how solid your strategic framework is, there will be surprises. You do your research and build out a clear business plan grounded in real data. You spend months preparing, identifying the best suppliers, targeting your customers, and putting everything in place. But when you open for business—when the vision becomes reality—there will be things you didn't anticipate. And how you respond will make all the difference.

The heavyweight champion Mike Tyson has a great saying that I love: "Everybody has a plan until they get punched in the mouth."[3] It applies to business as well as boxing: you do your homework, study your opponent, identify what you can do to win... and still, when you step into that ring, you're going to get punched. How do you respond to that first blow? Your ability to respond to adversity and to unanticipated events will dictate whether your business will succeed or quickly fold. Your framework can help you here as well. You want to build systems to help you endure and thrive, even in the midst of unexpected setbacks.

---

2. Marshall Goldsmith, "A 6-Part Structure for Giving Clear and Actionable Feedback," Harvard Business Review, August 7, 2015.

3. Mike Berardino, "Mike Tyson Explains One of His Most Famous Quotes," Sun Sentinel, September 28, 2021, https://www.sun-sentinel.com/sports/fl-xpm-2012-11-09-sfl-mike-tyson-explains-one-of-his-most-famous-quotes-20121109-story.html.

I recently participated in a two-day workshop for one of our latest ventures, a startup. The founding partner has been operating this business successfully in his home country and invited us into a partnership to set up the same business in Saudi Arabia.

We launched the business, but after three months, we hadn't realized the results that we had been expecting. In fact, we hadn't signed a single client.

I can imagine what you're thinking: No customers after three months? That's an event that might inspire panic, even among experienced entrepreneurs. But believe it or not, no one was in panic mode. We were confident in the research we had done and the structure we had put in place. We came together to brainstorm and discover what we could do to change these results. Where were we deviating from the successful original model? Were our initial assumptions incorrect?

As we worked systematically through each assumption, we realized that they were, in fact, correct. What we needed to adjust was our pricing structure. We examined the financials and recognized that we could tweak the pricing for our first ten clients. We needed to make that adjustment to attract those first critical customers; essentially, we agreed to take the hit in order to move the business forward. What we recognized was that those customers would enable us to demonstrate that we could deliver quality results; that track record should then lead to additional customers at our original pricing structure.

We didn't do this as an act of desperation. We used the data to build a model that showed how many customers we needed and how that reduced pricing would impact our overall budget and profit margin.

Because we were confident in our initial assumptions, we could keep a positive attitude as we worked to solve the problem. We knew that even though we didn't have that first client, it was a matter of not if, but when.

As an entrepreneur, you need to prepare for setbacks and challenges along the way, even at the beginning. There's always a fresh opportunity to go back to your framework, to identify what you didn't anticipate earlier, without being discouraged, and to make adjustments. I say make adjustments because even though you've invested months or even years in creating your business plan, you want to create a plan that is flexible, one that you can fine-tune as you operate your business and identify new opportunities and challenges. There will always be discoveries, especially during your first year of operation, things that you may not have known or understood as you were creating your model. There's always a new opportunity to ask yourself, If I make this change if I pivot because of this setback or new opportunity, do I still have a business? Is it a business that I want to run? Is it a business that will be profitable?

The last question is critical. If your business is not profitable, you can't stay the course. I'm saying this not to discourage you. Instead, I want to encourage you to check your ego at the door, to make sure that the decisions you're making will lead to what you've identified as success. You shouldn't make these decisions emotionally. You want to be objective, to go back to your initial assumptions and carefully review them without taking any setbacks personally.

Fashion entrepreneur Daymond John has spent much of his life building businesses and investing in entrepreneurial ventures. In an interview with Entrepreneur, he highlighted the framework he uses to assess startups and new launches: "When looking at trends I always ask myself basic and timeless questions about business, and the one I seem to always come back to is, 'How is this different than anything else in the marketplace?'"[4]

That question should be your North Star as you test your assumptions and evaluate what's next. Are you offering something different? Are you solving a problem in a way that is meaningful to you and profitable for your business?

How Do You Measure Success?

As an entrepreneur, I'm never satisfied. I'm always ready to explore new ideas and new opportunities. I want to be challenged. I began by wanting to run one business successfully. Today, I'm eager to run many different ventures in many different countries, scale existing businesses, and work with fellow entrepreneurs to create meaningful change in Saudi Arabia.

I was talking with a friend not too long ago, someone I've known for a long time who's also a successful CEO. He patiently listened to me chat about a specific goal for one of my businesses. I was sharing my wish to take this business globally, to move into the African and European markets. I wound up boldly stating my intent to generate enough income so that I could become a billionaire.

My friend didn't laugh at me. Instead, he asked, "Why? Why do you want to have a billion dollars?"

---

4. Shira Lazar, "Daymond John on Engaging Young Entrepreneurs and Building a Better Business," Entrepreneur (Entrepreneur, April 24, 2012), https://www.entrepreneur.com/leadership/daymond-jo hn-on-engaging-young-entrepreneurs-and-building-a/223409.

I quickly responded with a list of things I would use that money for, ambitious goals that were both personal and professional.

"Okay," he said, "let's calculate how much you actually need."

We took my list and went through it systematically, putting actual price tags on each item. By the end, I discovered that I didn't need a billion dollars to achieve all of my goals. I actually needed much, much less.

"That's your number," my friend told me. "That's how you measure success."

It was a powerful exercise, one that reinforced a message I've tried to share with you in this book. Vision is important for a business. Ambitious goals and dreams fuel your effort. But in the end, you need data. You need research that answers key questions. You need to know, clearly and specifically, how you will measure success.

For every entrepreneur, that measure is unique, one that reflects your individual goals. I encourage you to identify that measurement, to intentionally use it as a marker as you implement processes and track your progress.

For me, that billion-dollar figure I thought I needed was a way to ensure freedom and financial independence. Once I discovered that I could achieve what I had identified as fundamental to that freedom without a billion dollars, it transformed my decision-making. Without that artificial pressure, I discovered a different freedom— the ability to refine the goals for my business in ways that were more strategic and aligned with the frameworks I had developed.

It's a bit like looking at your destination from ten kilometers away. As you get closer to your destination, your vision goes from 2D to 3D. You gain clarity. You can see how that goal looks and experience how it feels.

I'm also getting better at celebrating small successes instead of just big achievements. My team takes plenty of hits. They have customers shouting at them, and suppliers complaining. When we hit a KPI, we take that moment to recognize it and celebrate it. It might be with a catered team lunch. It may be that we close down an hour earlier on Thursday to start our weekend a bit sooner (in Saudi Arabia, the workweek ends on Thursday, and Friday and Saturday are weekend days).

These may seem like little things, but for an entrepreneur, it's important to take that moment to pause and acknowledge what's been done well—to just say thank you to everyone who contributed. Those small wins lead to big wins.

Small wins lead to big wins.

I'm better at celebrating the team wins than the personal wins. Fortunately, I have a wonderful wife who reminds me of my successes and encourages me to celebrate them. I'm superstitious; I'm worried that if I celebrate a win too early, God will punish me! But what I've learned is that the best way to celebrate success is to experience gratitude. I track progress, and when I reach a milestone, I try to always take time to be grateful for what's been achieved and to share that with everyone who has contributed to the success.

There's interesting research from the Lloyd Greif Center for Entrepreneurial Studies at the University of Southern California's Marshall School of Business that suggests that gratitude is a key contributor to high-performing teams.[5] Grateful people are easier to work with, leading to a more productive organization. Leaders who demonstrate their gratitude create a stronger work environment. The study even shows fewer employee sick days when leaders demonstrate their gratitude!

So take that time to celebrate your wins with your team. Be thankful for what they've done, and express your gratitude to your employees, your suppliers, and your customers. Then look ahead to what's next.

---

5. Glenn Fox and Rebecca Castillo, "Profit with Gratitude: Building the Foundations of a Grateful Organization," Lloyd Greif Center for Entrepreneurial Studies, Marshall School of Business, USC, October 20, 2021

Part V
Close the Strategy-to-Execution Gap

Chapter Eight

How Will You Execute The Strategy?

"Let your joy be in your journey—not in some distant goal."

—TIM COOK

A Quick Recap

The chapters of this book have been structured around the crucial questions that entrepreneurs shall be answering when forming the strategic framework of their startups. Reflecting on (and answering) those questions made transformational changes in both my own businesses and in the startups where I played the role of an advisor and/or an angel investor.

Speaking from my own experiences, when my team and I first ever attempted to work on our organization's strategic framework, to our surprise, we discovered that what thought were strengths in our businesses were, in fact, weaknesses for the simple reason being our strategy wasn't clear to most people within the organization. We didn't spend time discussing our strategic framework as an executive team. I thought that it was obvious to everyone within the organization, but I learned that I needed to take specific steps to clarify the strategy for myself, for the executive team, and then for the entire organization.

When I talk about strategy, I'm talking about an action plan, a framework that a business will use to achieve its goals. Strategy in this sense is centered around profitability. It's the process you will use to create and sustain economic value. For an entrepreneur, it's vital to build and manage this framework.

Whenever I want to look at strategy execution, this list of questions shall be considered as the commandments an entrepreneur shall ask— and answer:

1. What's the problem you're trying to solve?

2. What is the market size?

3. Is this industry sustainable going forward?

4. Who is your ideal customer— and what specific value are you offering them?

5. How is the cash flowing?

6. Who are the people you need on your team?

7. What are the potential pitfalls to success?

8. How will you execute the strategy?

Let's start with the first question: *__What's the problem you're trying to solve?__* This takes us to the first chapter of this book where there was an emphasis on your ability, as an entrepreneur, to make clear yes/no choices to deliver a product or a service that will solve a real problem to your target audience and in a way that is economically sustainable. For you to focus on what matters, you need to learn to say "No" to other things. As Michael

Porter said eloquently in his quote "The essence of strategy is choosing what not to do."

Once you are clear on the problem you're trying to solve and you've identified the solution that your company (or startup) can deliver, you need to make the transition from problem-solving to operating a profitable business. This is when you need to ask yourself "***What is the market size?***" This requires gathering data and conducting some market research. At this stage, you need to be driven by numbers, and not by your feelings or your passion for your product or service. Data and market understanding will enable you to come up with realistic assumptions about your business; however, always remember to question your assumptions and that you're comfortable with the potential risk you might be undertaking.

Next, you need to determine whether "***this industry is sustainable going forward***". As you prepare to launch your business, explore a new venture, or grow and scale an existing business, it's vital to examine what is happening in your market and your industry. It's not simply a matter of preparing a list of developments and factors; it's analyzing and assessing how those events, those dynamics, will impact your business and your customers.

After focusing on the big picture—your industry—, you will need to transition to a more targeted assessment of how your business will create value. In other words, you need to ask yourself "***Who is your ideal customer—and what specific value are you offering them?***" You need to have clear answers on what difference you will make to your customers, and how you will make their life easier, more efficient, and better. When you know your customer deeply, it will become clear to you who is not your customer and which services or products are not real solutions to problems your target customers have.

The next level gets more granular. This is where the rubber meets the road. You need to have clear answers to the question *"**How is the cash flowing?**"* This means you need to have a solid understanding of the capital required to build a business that solves problems. Running out of cash will eventually lead to failure. The most successful entrepreneurs I've known focused less on the money they might make and more on the problems they can solve; however, they were on top of their business's financial health, they became profitable, and could continue to add value to their customers by solving their problems. Understanding cash flow will be critical for your business's success.

One of the most strategic decisions you will make as you launch your company comes as you begin to answer the question *"**Who are the people you need on your team?**"* As the leader of your business, allow your strategy to determine who will be right for you to hire, rather than allowing the people you've hired to determine the right strategy. Without fully understanding how you're going to compete and forming a clear financial picture, it's impossible to make strategic hiring decisions. The same strategy that has informed your decision-making throughout this process should be used as you determine who you need to contribute to your success— your A players.

If your response to the question *"**What are the potential pitfalls to success?**"* is an enthusiastic "Nothing!" I encourage you to remember that confidence is good, but strategy is even better. I've found it very helpful to identify potential challenges and prepare for them in advance. I want to respond ahead of time to any significant obstacles to success, whether that means ensuring that I have a broad network of suppliers or working to retain my best employees.

Once you've answered the first seven questions, you can tackle the eighth *"How will you execute the strategy?"*

How Will You Execute the Strategy?

My experience in my businesses and my engagements with the many entrepreneurs I often engage with taught me that every startup needs to identify three to five top priorities to help the founders (or executive team) focus on the most critical elements that will impact their ability to succeed.

If you're a new entrepreneur, think about the markers that will be vital to your successful launch in year one, and your growth in years two and three. Is there a specific contract you must win or a target group of customers you need to reach? If so, that's where you'll want to frame your strategy.

The questions that form the chapters of this book will enable you to break down strategy into small pieces and to think realistically about how those pieces connect to you and your business. The questions seem simple at first glance, but they quickly become deep as you begin to answer them.

The process of answering them might take time. For our team, each question took about two months of workshops just to answer thoroughly and properly. But it was a very effective way to ensure that our team was in alignment. The worst thing I think any business can do is rely on assumptions—or even build assumptions on assumptions—rather than facts. When you begin to answer these questions, when you put them down on paper or on a whiteboard, or on a tablet, you can begin to assess where those answers are coming from. What is the source of the assumption you've made? How true is it? Does it resonate with the rest of your team?

Seek the Help of Advisors

I realize that some entrepreneurs may be operating solo ventures at the beginning, but this is an opportunity to enlist the help of a mentor or advisor. Share your answers to these questions and ask them for feedback. See if they agree with the assumptions you've made, and if not, determine why.

Getting Ready to Talk to an Advisor

As you're putting together your business plan or investors' pitch deck, you want to make sure you're answering those five questions throughout the plan. If you want to approach an angel investor or a venture capital to fund your startup, I assure you they have those set of questions on their mind, among other questions they're interested in. If potential investors will sense the founder or the founding team didn't think and answer those questions, it will be a sign of a flawed plan and their interest in listening to your plan will seriously be diminished.

To me, this is a very powerful tool. Many of the challenges our businesses have experienced have stemmed from incorrect assumptions. Answering these questions puts all of those assumptions into the open, so there's no hidden agenda and no superficial responses to plans or processes. You have to dig down deep.

Enjoy the Journey

The process of launching a business can be all-consuming. For months, even years, you dream about what you want to accomplish and how you will accomplish it. You research and plan and prepare.

It doesn't get easier when your business is launched. You'll spend long hours fine-tuning your plans once the business is a reality, identifying what's working and what needs to change. You make that critical transition from an entrepreneur to a leader of a thriving venture and quite possibly begin planning for what's next.

Allow me to share a bit of advice with you as this book comes to an end: Entrepreneurship is a journey. Not every venture will succeed—in fact, many will not. It's important to recognize that with each start and stop you learn, you build your expertise, and you discover how to be better with the next venture.

It's popular to talk about work/life balance, and I confess that I have yet to identify what that ideal balance looks like. When I first started out as an entrepreneur, I was a single guy hanging out with a lot of other friends who were either starting their own businesses or moving into a family business. We had a lot in common, and we'd stay out late at night talking about what we would do, how we would change the business world, and generally dreaming big about the influence we would have. We were all beginning that entrepreneurial journey together, and it was great to have that network of friends with so many similarities and so much we could share. It was a reminder that we weren't alone. We created a circle of trust and could discuss successes and failures with others whose experiences were similar.

Things changed when members of the group started getting married—including me. We used to work all day and then spend late nights talking about work, but my priorities began to shift once I had a wife and then a family. Suddenly, I was no longer juggling business and friendships; instead, I was juggling business, friendships, and family.

When you're juggling, it's challenging to keep two balls in the air. But when you add that third ball, it becomes significantly more difficult. One ball is in your hand, one ball is always in the air, and the third is at risk of being dropped.

The ball I let go of was my friendships. I spent more time with my wife and kids and focused intently on my businesses. I no longer spent time with peers, sharing experiences, celebrating successes, and commiserating over failures. I no longer had that constant network helping to brainstorm solutions to challenges I was encountering.

It's a natural phenomenon, an understandable set of priorities. But after about ten years, I was at an event in Australia, and a colleague told me that he wanted to introduce me to a friend of his. He thought we had a lot in common and would benefit from talking to each other. We met up and ended up talking for four or five hours.

Because we were in Australia, I had the flexibility—away from the office and away from my family—to just focus on building that connection. Because of the time difference between Australia and Saudi Arabia, my phone was quiet. I wasn't distracted by the need to rush off for a meeting or interrupted by calls or messages.

We were working in different fields, so there was no sense of competition. We could share challenges and ideas from the perspective of two CEOs who are interested in learning from each other.

We built a friendship from that first meeting. We've continued to meet and chat as often as possible, and those conversations have been very helpful—they've enabled me to get fresh eyes on a problem and discuss possible outcomes with an unbiased but expert listener. Recently, this friend shared a story that really touched me. He works in wealth management, and he told me that his clients often request dinner meetings. The majority of the wealthy individuals who want his expertise ask to meet in the evenings rather than during the workday. The reason, my friend discovered, is because they are lonely.

During working hours, they are surrounded by employees, but they've dedicated so much time and attention to building up the wealth in their business that they've lost touch with the friends with whom they could share a meal or a cup of coffee.

What a sad story, I thought when he first shared it with me. And then I paused and reflected. What was I doing to strengthen my social network, to connect not only with professional colleagues but with friends? I felt energized after chatting with my friend, but he lives in a different part of the world, so the opportunities we have to share a meal and a conversation are limited. I had spent so many hours building my businesses and caring for my family that I had forgotten to prioritize friendships as well.

I'm working to correct this and to build my social leadership skill—to take actions designed to cultivate stronger networks outside my home and workplace. I encourage you to do the same, to cultivate those friendships outside your workplace. Those are the friends who will give you honest feedback, celebrate your achievements, and if necessary, help you remember your goals and refocus.

There's a saying in Arabic: Heaven is worthless with no friends. That saying has inspired me to rethink my priorities or at least ensure that friendships actually become one of my priorities. As an entrepreneur, you should build a business that can survive without you. You want to create a venture that has lasting value. If you can't take an hour or two to attend a birthday party or take a day or two to fly to visit a friend or family member, you may need to reassess how healthy your business is.

The entrepreneurial journey should always include those pit stops, those opportunities to celebrate what you've created and enjoy its success. You should build a business in which you can trust other people to do the right thing. You should measure your success not simply on how much you make or the title you hold but on the individuals you've empowered and the opportunities you've created to live fully and joyfully.

I've discovered that there are really two pieces to the idea of work/life balance. One piece is paying attention to your social networks, and keeping them rich and healthy. The other is simply staying connected to who you are as a person—not just as an entrepreneur but as a human being. When you have a free evening or weekend, do you have people to hang out with? Does every conversation you have centered around your business?

I didn't like how I was answering those questions not long ago. Honestly, it's much easier to make friends when you're in school! Connections seemed to form more naturally in school or university; those environments are places where it's simpler to find others with whom you have something in common, whether it's a class or a major, or a sport you enjoy. As an entrepreneur, you most often meet with employees, suppliers, or customers. There's a different agenda that brings you together, and it's not necessarily an environment that leads to deep friendships.

What I'm discovering is the value of dedicating time to participating in organizations like YPO. Whatever field your startup is in, there's likely a group of professionals meeting somewhere. There are many of these groups specifically for Saudi entrepreneurs, offering meetups and opportunities to discuss strategy and share resources.

At one YPO regional event, I noticed someone's iPad. This guy was very professional and polished. He was doing a great job networking and handing out business cards, and I may even have felt a bit intimidated by his confidence. But then I saw that he had a Green Lantern logo on his iPad. Now, I'm a self-described geek, so I said something to him about the Green Lantern, and we quickly discovered that we had several things in common.

The next time I was in Dubai, I called him and told him that I had some time free at 7:30 a.m. for breakfast or 2:00 p.m. for a visit to the shooting range. He responded that he wanted to kick up his game in the shooting range, so we spent an hour shooting at clay pigeons and trying to be macho men. By the time the hour was over, that connection had become a friend, and we're very good friends to this day.

I've formed friendships around a shared love of cars and other activities. It's not all business, and those relationships where I invest just a little bit of time always create value. It may simply be time away from my desk doing something fun. It may be brainstorming or problem-solving. I don't like big networks; I like smaller groups and friendships that go beyond simply wishing someone happy birthday once a year.

I understand, believe me, that when you're an entrepreneur who's starting a business, it's challenging to do anything except that business. You may be thinking something like, "That sounds great. I'll do that in five years when the business is up and running." I know that feeling, and my purpose here isn't to tell you that one way is the right choice or the wrong choice. I'm just encouraging you not to forget why you've become an entrepreneur and to stay connected to the people who matter.

The Ten Skills You'll Need to Be an Entrepreneurial Leader

One of the challenges I've set for myself is to always improve and to grow as a leader as I'm growing my businesses. Whether it's building my social connections, identifying areas of improvement, or learning new skills, I'm always discovering new ways to push myself to be better.

Dr. Sunnie Giles, an organizational scientist and leadership development consultant, has studied 195 leaders in fifteen countries and asked them to choose the leadership competencies they recognized as most critical.[1]

Their list has helped me identify priorities for my own leadership development. You may find some surprises on this top ten list:

1. Has high ethical and moral standards.

2. Provides goals/objectives with loose guidelines/direction.

3. Clearly communicates expectations.

4. Has the flexibility to change opinions.

5. Is committed to my ongoing training.

---

1. Sunnie Giles, "The Most Important Leadership Competencies, According to Leaders around the World," Harvard Business Review, March 15, 2016.

6. Communicates often and openly.

7. Is open to new ideas and approaches.

8. Creates a feeling of succeeding and failing together.

9. Helps me grow into a next-generation leader.

10. Provides safety for trial and error.

When I'm meeting with fellow entrepreneurs, it's not all cheering each other on and extending a hand. No, when you get a group of entrepreneurs together, 99 percent of the time it will be competitive! I've found it helpful to set the tone from the beginning to try to remove a bit of that competitive edge. I start by acknowledging the other person's success. We talked earlier about the importance of a strategic framework, and honestly, the same structure can be helpful here. Ask yourself this question: What are you trying to accomplish? If you're trying to prove that you're more successful, then, by all means, go ahead. If your goal is to make a connection, to add this person to your network, think beyond their public persona to the real person beneath the surface.

Whether it's YPO, a professional club, or a network of entrepreneurs like the International Entrepreneurs' Organization, the best part of these groups is that it shouldn't matter who is more successful. Your purpose in participating in an organization like this is to grow as a professional, make connections, and build your network. You're all there to grow together—a great way to defuse that sense of competitiveness that seems to come naturally for those of us who are entrepreneurs.

What's Your Goal?

I talked earlier about the friend who challenged me to identify my true number, who pushed past my statement that I wanted to make a billion dollars to help me identify my actual goal. I challenge you to do the same thing when it comes to your goals for your business. My encouragement is for you to be clear about your goals, whether it's a number or some other marker of success.

Understanding your number—or your goal—comes back to the simple strategy of knowing what you're trying to achieve and identifying the true steps to get there. Suppose I'm starting a coffee shop and I say that my goal is to be the next Starbucks. What I need to do is unpack that goal to discover what I really want to accomplish. Do I want to have coffee shops all over the world? Do I want to earn a Starbucks level of revenue? Do I want to have that kind of brand recognition or serve that range of food and beverage items or create a similar atmosphere in my store? Do I truly need to check all those boxes, or do I really want to have three shops and a network of loyal and satisfied customers who come back again and again to drink my coffee?

Those are the goals that will shape your strategic model. That model will ensure that your aspirations are well-matched with your preparation and your process.

I try to work out, but I tend to get in much better shape when I have a specific goal in mind. Maybe I want to compete in a race, or I've competed and I want to improve my time or increase my upper-body strength. If you have a clear and specific target, it's much easier to get motivated to get to the gym. That works more than setting a general goal of spending thirty minutes on the treadmill or cross-training for an hour every day.

I'll ask you again: What's your goal? What will be the sign that you've achieved what you wanted to achieve and that you can celebrate your success? Spend some time thinking about this and writing it down. Knowing your goals will make it easier to say yes to certain things and no to others.

I encourage you to also think about your purpose—your mission, the reason you wake up every day. What matters to you? What impact do you want to have on the world? Hubert Joly, the former chairman and CEO of Best Buy, talks about the importance of purposeful leadership, noting that today's successful leaders are focused on recognizing what drives them and the people around them, and then using that motivation to create energy and momentum. It is important to recognize your motivation—your purpose—and then assess how the goal you've identified connects to this bigger purpose.

What matters to you? What impact do you want to have on the world?

When I talk to other entrepreneurs, we often find ourselves discussing what's next. The next business. The next opportunity. We're never satisfied.

Perhaps you're a bit like this. Perhaps you understand that ambition and drive.

As fellow entrepreneurs, we have a tremendous opportunity in Saudi Arabia. My encouragement to you is to be clear on your goal and your destination, but also to enjoy the journey. Celebrate every mile. Recognize how far you've come. And have people around you who will remind you of what truly matters.

Conclusion

AS AN ENTREPRENEUR, I'm always eager to look ahead, anticipate what the future will hold, and form a strategic framework to respond. Each framework I create is unique, reflecting different goals, different businesses, and even different industries.

But the core questions at the heart of the framework are the same. Whenever I start a business, I begin by identifying a problem I want to solve. I consider Rebecca Homkes's questions, asking, What's the situation? Where will we compete? How will we succeed? What's going to stop us? What should we do?

I build a strategy based on my answers to those questions. That strategy is shaped by the data I gather on market share, industry dynamics, and customer strategy, as well as my finances. I determine the right people to hire for my goals and identify how to monitor my progress.

Most of all, I do my best to enjoy the journey.

And now, it's your turn. It's your turn to build your own strategic framework to start your business. All businesses go through cycles, from startup to growth to reinvention. Your business may require different tools. You'll have your own unique mission and your own specific goals. But the fundamentals are the same.

I've focused on these fundamentals in this book and shared what I've learned through trial and error and by studying some of the top business strategists in the hope that these insights will equip you to succeed.

I'm continuing to learn, study, test out new approaches, and—yes—explore new businesses. I wanted this book to be practical, something you can take with you and refer back to at each stage of your business. There are so many topics I couldn't touch upon in a book this size—concepts like leadership, pricing, and marketing. I encourage you to keep learning and to keep exploring these and other areas that will help you to be successful as your business grows.

I can't wait to see what you'll achieve and to celebrate the launch of so many new businesses. I hope that this book is just the beginning of an ongoing conversation about what it takes to start and grow a successful business.

Your Invitation to Connect with Me and Book an Advisory Session

This book has come to its end and I invite you to take action on each of the concepts discussed. You may have taken action as you were reading the book. If not, I recommend you read it again and apply the learning. I can't stress this enough.

Once your plan is properly shaped up, you may still have many questions on how to go about certain challenges, access needed resources, get connected with the right partners or suppliers, find co-founders, get legal advice, or get funded for the seed or growth stage. I am happy to join you on a call where I will act as your startup advisor, challenge your idea, help you develop it further, point you in the right direction, or show interest in funding your startup. Below is a link to my calendar where you can book an Advisory Session with me:

https://calendly.com/husamalsaleh/business-startup-pitch

I also invite you to connect with me:

- LinkedIn: www.linkedin.com/in/husamsalsaleh

- Email: Husam.alsaleh@gmail.com

In whatever way you prefer to connect, make sure to mention "The Successful Business Startup Action Guide" so that I know what has inspired you to reach out.

I look forward to learning how the concepts I've shared in this book have impacted your entrepreneurial journey.

To your success...

About The Author

HUSAM IS A PASSIONATE, determined, and moral entrepreneur who has spent his career solving problems. Showing an entrepreneurial spirit at a young age, Husam often built solutions to the problems facing his friends and colleagues. He worked up the corporate ladder and became Deputy CEO of Arabian Hala Group, then continued his higher executive education at London Business School, Harvard Business School, IMD, and the MISK 2030 Leaders Program. This gave him the necessary skills to continue making solutions to problems in the market. Husam now holds several executive board positions, including CEO.

A key area of strength for him is startups, helping turn businesses around from loss to profit with a focus on growth. He leads his companies with inspiration in a shared mission and by bridging relationships with the main objective of creating something that will last.

Acknowledgments

WHEN I STARTED writing this book, it made me reflect on my journey. It made me feel humbled, and lucky to have a group of people around me who have shaped me.

I would like to start with my father. He has been an inspiration when it comes to true entrepreneurial spirit thanks to his grit and positive outlook on life. I will truly be grateful for those traits that continue to grow within me.

My mother has always made me appreciate the pursuit of knowledge. She pushes me to achieve more than what I think I'm capable of doing, and she has always done it with love and care.

My brother, Hani, has been more than just a sibling; he's a mentor, cheerleader, and, above all, a friend. I owe a lot of my knowledge, mistakes, and overachievement to him.

My sisters, Dania and Basmah, keep showing me how to enjoy life while still doing what you love.

Dr. Rebecca Homkes is the person who started me on the path to look at how to create frameworks that work, and I have learned a lot from her during the years, and I continue to add to her teachings.

Finally, I could not have written this book without the support of my wife, Nafla. She has been with me through the highs and lows. She has been my cornerstone, she has been my sounding board, and has been and continues to be my biggest supporter.

www.ingramcontent.com/pod-product-compliance
Lightning Source LLC
Chambersburg PA
CBHW071418210326
41597CB00020B/3566